I am so deeply stirred by my dear friend L̲ erful new book, *Crowns Are Greater Than Trophies*. I believe this is a sage is for all generations! This book is a message from the throne of heaven delivered to the bride with compassion, love, truth, and wisdom. It will stir you to go deeper in Jesus, rebuild the altar of the Lord, and die to everything that has held you back. This is a "yet, even now" book! I personally know the man well, and I love the message that God has entrusted to the messenger. This book is destined to be a classic for all those called to carry the cross!

—Pat Schatzline
Evangelist and Author of *Rebuilding the Altar*
and Why IS God So Mad at Me?
Remnant Ministries International

With creative metaphors that align with the purpose of supernatural personal growth, Timothy McCain writes of a cultural clash with wit and wisdom. Tim attacks the fallacies of a corrupted society with the authority of God's word. This book will push you to expose the enemy's effect on Christianity with sound spiritual development and practical insight. Grab a cup of coffee and get your heart ready for supernatural fuel. You will accelerate beyond your current capacity and attain another dimension of God's best for your life!

—Evangelist Allen Griffin
www.AgMinistries.com
Author of the book *Undefeated*

Timothy McCain is a "thought leader" for our generation. His hard hitting truths in *Crowns Are Greater Than Trophies* gets right to the heart of the cancer that's taking out a generation of leaders. Reading and application of this book give world changers the ammunition they need to fight one of the most important battles of their lives. I recommend this book to everyone who has an ounce of influence and a desire to do good. This could save your life.

—Mike Rosas
National Speaker, NBA
Houston Rockets Chaplain

In his new book, Timothy McCain brilliantly extracts life-changing truths from the word of God who every believer needs to hear. Too many have allowed the pursuit of "trophies" to steal their focus, causing an unhealthy and dysfunctional Christian walk. *Crowns Are Greater Than Trophies* speaks directly to what is crippling so many today, and offers the hope of restoration so needed in our culture!

—Pastor Matt Engle
Mainstream High School Youth Pastor
Faith Assembly of God, Orlando FL

Timothy McCain gets to the heart of the matter of many of society's issues in *Crowns Are Greater Than Trophies*. This book cuts past the peripheral symptoms and strikes at the very core of the problematic and systemic root of mankind's affair with self-gratification. Not only is it an intriguing snapshot of some of history's darkest moments, but it provides the answers for hope and true generational change.

—Jamie Jones
Pastor of Trinity Church Deltona, FL,
and author of *The Left-Handed Warrior*

Evangelist Timothy McCain has written a powerful book that our generation needs to read. In his chapter titled "The Year That Pride Died," it teaches how to intentionally protect yourself against pride by starving it with humility. Wow! *Crowns Are Greater Than Trophies* will undo generations of curses that may be plaguing you or your family. Invest in your future and your legacy by reading this book.

—Joshua McCain
Worship Pastor at Trinity Church, Deltona, FL

Crowns are Greater than Trophies, has the potential to shine a spotlight of hope and extend a lifeline of deliverance to its readers. There is a generational chain that is about to be broken off of our lives, with the help of the Holy Spirit and the work of Jesus, for the glory of God. These pages are about to empower the reader with the anointing to restore to this generation the understanding that we are not to boast about ourselves; if we want to boast, then we are to proclaim the glories of God (1 Cor. 1:31; 2 Cor. 10:17). Timothy's book gives us a portal through which the almighty God can flow down to us, and then out through us.

—Doug Sayers
Pennsylvania/Delaware
Youth Ministries Director Assemblies of God

I often hear, "How can a book written thousands of years ago relate to where I am at today?" Well, Evangelist Timothy McCain has showed us once again the reality that the word of God is timeless. The same core principles the enemy has used might be masked in a different costume today, but the core heart issues are still at work. We *must* recognize the enemy of our souls is after our hearts the same today as in years past. This book does a spectacular job of opening our eyes to one of the enemy's most common methods that he employs to pull us from the heart of God. If there is ever a book this generation needs to digest, *Crowns Are Greater Than Trophies* is that book. My desire is that this book is not just read but consumed!

—Rev. Joshua Grimes
Regional Executive Director
for Open Bible East

I first met Pastor Timothy McCain when he spoke to the Nyack College student body, challenging them to be real in their relationships with God, and I have followed his life and ministry with great interest ever since. He is a fresh and needed voice for the times we live, someone unique in his ability to convey the eternal truths of scripture in relevant and tangible ways. If you dare to follow these pages, this book will lead you deeper into the heart of God, where all who enter never remain the same.

—Dan Bailey
Director of Admission Nyack College, Rockland Campus

I have been working in church leadership for fifty-two years. Seldom have I known anyone with a passion for Jesus like Timothy McCain. This book conveys that passion, using a story that is familiar but powerful. Hopefully it will convey that passion to you!

—Dr. Dennis Robinson
President, League of Christian Schools, Headmaster,
Trinity Christian Academy, and Professor,
Southwestern Assemblies of God University

Evangelist Timothy McCain delivers a powerful challenge to the readers of this epic book, *Crowns Are Greater Than Trophies*. You will be encouraged to establish and restore an altar in your home. Your children will be able to come boldly daily at your table and receive deliverance and instructions in righteousness. As Evangelist Timothy McCain pours his heart out, you feel the anointing in his writing!

—Honorable Minister Webster Barnaby
Former City Commissioner Deltona, Florida

This book has a powerful message that is so important for this generation to grasp. In a world where we crave acknowledgement and praise, this book comes at the perfect time. *Crowns Are Greater Than Trophies* is a life-changing read!

—Kristen Alvarez
Founder and CEO of Lovedearly.org

At a time when so many struggle to stay focused on the priorities of spiritual growth that stand the test of time, Timothy calls the Church to humility of life, awareness of subtle compromise, and passionate discipleship. His message and personal journey will challenge you and inspire you to withstand the forces of a culture that would seek to draw the hearts of leaders and their flocks away from the heart of God.

—Don Williams,
Lead Pastor, First Missionary Church, Berne, IN

I just finished reading excerpts from my friend, Evangelist Timothy McCain's new book "Crowns Are Greater Than Trophies". I am excited about this new work and its impact on all who dare to read it. Tim moves from scripture to life in a smooth and effective way. He highlights the confusion that often comes when we begin to push for trophies – the things that elevate us, rather than crowns – the things that glorify Christ. This book addresses those of us who love Jesus and ministry, but also the seductive rewards that can come from a misplaced love of accolades from ministry and the crowd. Timothy brings an honest heart and sobering look at how we serve the King and the care that must constantly be given in our use of time, talent and skills. At every turn of a chapter, I sensed the convicting presence of Christ calling us to higher living, making sure that we do not build our lives upon sand even while sharing Christ with others. I am so proud of Timothy and grateful for a job well done. The wisdom shared will make us all better servants of Christ.

—Pastor Ron Hawkins
Senior Pastor, First Assembly of God, Fort Wayne, Indiana

CROWNS ARE GREATER THAN TROPHIES

CROWNS ARE GREATER THAN TROPHIES

Confronting Pride and Uprooting Entitlement by Cultivating a Servant's Heart

Timothy McCain

Xulon Press
2301 Lucien Way #415
Maitland, FL 32751
407.339.4217
www.xulonpress.com

Unless otherwise indicated, Scripture quotations taken from the
King James Version (KJV) – public domain, the Holy Bible, New
International Version (NIV). Copyright © 1973, 1978, 1984, 2011 by
Biblica, Inc.™. Used by permission. All rights reserved, the New King
James Version (NKJV). Copyright © 1982 by Thomas Nelson, Inc.
Used by permission. All rights reserved.

Printed in the United States of America.

ISBN-13: 978-1-54563-987-0

DEDICATION

I dedicate this book to my beautiful wife Madai and my son Hezekiah. Madai, I love you more than tacos with a tamarindo Jarritto. Thank you for being such an encourager to me as I wrote this book and being my bride. I love traveling the world with you, preaching and sharing the gospel. Hezekiah, you are my joy in the flesh and make me want to be a better person every day. I love being your daddy. You are a conqueror and a world changer. I love you both.

In memory of
Pastor Mike Connis

CONTENTS

FOREWORD

First Peter 2:9 says, "But ye are a chosen generation, a royal priesthood, an holy nation, a peculiar people; that ye should shew forth the praises of him who hath called you out of darkness into his marvelous light." and Second Corinthians 4:7 says "But we have this treasure in earthen vessels, that the excellency of the power may be of God, and not of us."

When I consider these scriptures and many others that are given by inspiration of God, I am convinced that *you*, the reader of this amazing book, have been *marked* by God for a purpose so much greater than you could ever realize or understand. You've been pre-destined for greatness and designed for success. You have been created to be a world changer and a history maker. God's hand of power is on your life. There is no question that God has brought you into the kingdom for such a time as this.

You are creative, talented, and innovative, and are full of dreams, passions, ideas, and desires that, when manifested in fullness, will cause an amazing harvest of souls. People will be inspired to walk in their God-given assignment as they see you walking and thriving in yours. You have the power to get wealth. You have been graced with influence. Leadership is in your DNA. You walk in dominion and authority.

People follow you and love it! When you speak, people listen. When you start walking in any direction, you have a following. It's a *God-given* grace that is upon your life. You didn't ask for it; God did it. It's amazing that God has raised you up in this generation.

As incredible as this is, it is this very reason why the enemy will attack you with pride and selfish ambition, and cause you to make your visions and dreams "idols" that you worship; he will even try to make God a servant to your ambitions and endeavors. This amazing book—*Crowns Are Greater Than Trophies* is a *must read* for people like us. God has raised up Timothy McCain to send a "gut check" to the body of Christ, especially those anointed by God to lead. If you don't think you need a gut check in these areas, that's the *biggest indicator* that you need to read this book in full.

Many of us will bypass crowns to chase trophies. This is because we struggle with identity and value. Crowns aren't earned; they are inherited through sonship. Trophies are earned through human effort. Although there is absolutely nothing wrong with having a trophy, there is something terribly wrong when a trophy, or the idea of having a trophy, *has you*! *Crowns Are Greater Than Trophies* will help you discover where you are as it relates to this. Remember this: you don't accomplish anything to gain an identity or to find value. If you did *nothing*, your identity and value would not change. You have been crowned with glory and honor because you are the son of the King of kings. Your trophies are the byproduct of the crown of sonship you already possess.

As you read *Crowns Are Greater Than Trophies*, allow the Holy Spirit to search your heart and purify you of all motives, intentions, ambitions, and unhealthy passions that God never wanted or intended for you. May you realize who you are and that God loves the authentic you that He created!"

Pastor Eddie James
www.EddieJames.com

ACKNOWLEDGMENTS

My family Kenneth, Lillian, Damien, Christina, Lillie, Jacob, Pastor Joshua, Jonathan, and extended family.
Pastors Jamie and Michelle Jones
Staff members of Trinity Church and Trinity Christian Academy
The members of Trinity Church of Deltona, Florida
Pastors Kim and Connie Snyder
The staff and members of First Assembly of God in Asheboro
Pastors Ron and Joy Hawkins
The staff and members of First Assembly of God in Fort Wayne, Indiana
Evangelists Allen and Hashmareen Griffin
Evangelists Pat and Karen Schatzline
Amy Pratt
Pastors Steve and Elaine Furr
Pastors Karl and Cindy Fleig
Bart and Leslie Singer and family
Rick and Sherrie Brooks
Pastors Eugene and Felicia Davis
Bishop Tony and Kathy Miller
Pastors Terry and Debra Howell
Pastors Jim and Dawn Riley
Pastors Remi and Valerie and Family
The Stensland family

D. J. Armstrong
Alan and Theresa Lance
Tom and Dora Hoelle
Pastors Don and Nancy Williams
Pastors Barry and Tami Jorris
Pastors Matthew and Sydney Hammersky
Dr. James and Kymala Johnson
Dr. David and Hedi Choie
Fredrick Maiocco and Family
Pastors Steve and Elaine Furr
Herb Rapp
Evangelist Wayne and Rita Perdue
Ben Hall
James Rivers and family
Greg and Pam Small
Mark and Ronda Trollinger
Pastors Jay and Kimberly Nicoson
Pastors Jim and Janet Turner
Pastors Andy and Sheryl Weil
Pastors Pedro and Sharon Muniz
Pastor Santos Rivera
Pastor Holly Noe
Dennis Williams
Pastors Gabriel and Tami Trevino
Pastors Jeff and Julie Edmonson
Pastors Jay and Debi Burnett
The members of Calvary Chapel of Pasadena, Texas
Pastors Chad and Julie McAtee
Pastors Corey and Karesha Shiver
Pastors Dave and Tara Snyder
The Whippo Family
Nyack College
North Carolina Masters Commission

CHAPTER 1

THREE CROWNS, SAME TROPHY

I will never forget the time I almost died. I was heading back from a party with two other friends in my old and barely running beat-up car. I grew up in North Carolina, and the terrain is covered with steep hills and busy traffic. I was leaned back in the driver's seat as if I was shooting a hip-hop music video. It would have been cool to say that we were listening to music, grooving our heads to the beat, but the radio didn't work. We were cruising down the road with the windows rolled down because I didn't have an air conditioner, either. I turned on a long and steep road called Highway 14 when I experienced a life-changing event. I started driving downhill when I noticed that I was picking up speed, so I pressed my brakes to slow down. All of a sudden, I realized that we were all in trouble.

I pushed on the brakes a couple of other times to make sure I wasn't mistaken. My fear was correct; my brakes weren't working. In a nonchalant tone, I told the guys with me that my brakes weren't working. At first, they thought I was joking until they quickly saw that the car was picking up speed fast, and I was slamming on the brakes, but the car wasn't slowing down. All of a sudden, the hardcore "mean mug" glaring fellow's facial expressions changed into a state of panic. We were flying down a steep highway in what we knew would be our mobile coffin. To add to the alarm, at the end of the hill was an intersection, and our light just turned red. The car was like a speeding bullet directed toward its doomed target. We approached the intersection, and a tractor trailer rolled into my lane, I swerved quickly and missed it. Every car that I dodged was a near-death experience. To make matters worse, we were heading toward a bridge, which was hovering over a long drop above the water.

In the midst of a fear-induced and adrenaline-fueled moment, I felt I had no choices. I couldn't slow down in the least, thus making it impossible to stop. Knowing that this was going to be the last moment of my life, I mentally prepared myself that I was going to die. However, what happened next completely opened my eyes to see the divine intervention of God. All of a sudden, as we were flying toward the side of the bridge, my car stopped. It was as if God did the "parent arm." You know the parent arm, right? It's the time when you were in the passenger seat and your parents had to slam on the brakes, and they would instinctively stretch out their arm to keep you from flying out of your seat. With all confidence, I know that God stopped the car and not only saved my life but also the lives of my two friends that day.

I stepped out of the car thankful for life and greatly confused. I pondered, "What happened to my car that the brakes would completely give out like that?" I thought that it was a detailed series of events or somehow my brake lines were cut as if we were starring in the next Final Destination movie. Little did I know that a simple act of negligence almost cost us our lives. I called my dad to let him know about the series of events and to troubleshoot the issues. He asked me a direct and straightforward question that put everything into perspective. "Did you check the brake fluid"? I opened the hood and checked the reservoir, and it was bone dry. It wasn't a complicated string of events that ushered me into circumstances having the potential to take life but a simple act of negligence. Often in life, the falsely perceived "little things" can have massive impacts. The problem that I ignored had death as its consequence.

Songs of Solomon 2:15 says, "Catch us the foxes, the little foxes that spoil the vines, for our vines have tender grapes."

The book of Second Chronicles lists a generation of kings who had all fallen into the same pattern of behavior. They had followed transitional and adopted mindsets that were seen modeled before them and that had been passed down to them. These kings did terrific exploits for God and the people who they were entrusted to rule. However, in the mist of their lives was an unknown thread that time pulled upon and pride grasped that unraveled their legacy. They started off well, but they didn't end well. They were kings who didn't check their brake fluid; they were kings who were running but refused to stop.

Long Live the King

The start of King Joash's life was that of a suspense movie. The king before him, named Ahaziah, started his reign at the young adult age of twenty-two years old. Ahaziah didn't rule under the guidance of biblical standards and Godly teachings. He wasn't a man of God who desired to uphold God-centered principles, but he ruled in an evil manner. The people of influence around him were destructive voices who would entertain and adopt the wicked behavior that King Ahaziah would also later commit.

2 Chronicles 22:3–4

He too followed the ways of the house of Ahab, for his mother encouraged him to act wickedly. He did evil in the eyes of the Lord, as the house of Ahab had done, for after his father's death they became his advisers, to his undoing.

His reign was cut short as many plotted against him to kill him. These acts were achieved when he went to visit Jehu, son of Nimshi, who was the one anointed by God to end his wicked reign. After King Ahaziah's mother Athaliah heard of her son's death, she went on a rampage. She destroyed the entire royal family of the House of Judah and would have killed the future King Joash, but mercy stepped in. The daughter of King Jehoram rescued the future king by stealing him and hiding him in a bedroom at the temple along with his nurse. They continued hiding from Athaliah and remained in the temple for six years. King Joash literally grew up in the temple. He was raised at "church." King Joash dwelled in the place where worship used to happen. He grew up in the house of God. That place of worship was literally his sanctuary, his place of refuge and protection. How much can we learn today knowing that we have protection and comfort in the rest and sanctuary of almighty God? "God is our refuge and strength, an ever-present help in trouble" (Psalm 46:1 NIV).

Unlike his predecessor, he was raised with the voice of Godly wisdom and people who had his best interests in mind. A man who played a critical role in his life was a priest named Jehoiada. The man of God protected him, fought for him, and paved a way so that he could live without the fear of impending death at every turn. Jehoiada went on a mission to restore what was broken and taken away. He made covenants with commanders, all of whom made a covenant and promise with the king at the temple. King Joash was blessed to have people in his life but didn't expect anything in return.

Priest Jehoiada mobilized the remnant of priests and Levites and stationed them at different tactical locations. He placed some guarding the doors on the Sabbath. A third of the meek warriors he placed at the royal palace and the other third taking watch at the Foundation Gate. Everyone left in the gathering of committed believers were sent to the courtyard of the temple. Just as a herd of animals would create a circle and barrier around their children to protect them, so the priests were attempting to do for King Joash. The Levites were positioned around the king, with weapons ready and strict instructions that whoever steps foot into the temple without authorization was to be put to death. The mission to protect the king was paramount. The Levites were the Secret Service agents for King Joash, bound by a covenant to do or sacrifice whatever was necessary for his wellbeing and safety.

Finally, a day that Jehoiada and the Levites paved a way for had arrived. That day should have been a moment in history that would break the pattern of wicked rule. It was a colossal occasion that was seven years in the making and a place in history paved in blood and sacrifice. The faithful servants of God, Jehoiada and his sons, ushered the king into a day he would never forget. Joash was finally crowned as king. One of the sons present during King Joash crowning was the soon-to-be Prophet Zechariah. As they placed the crown on his heard, they gave him a copy of the covenant, a copy of the promise and commitment they have made.

They anointed him as king and decreed and shouted, "Long live the King!" What an occasion for Priest Jehoiada and everyone connected to ushering this event. All the sweat, blood, and tears it took to see the leadership and vision shifted was finally fulfilled. The nation was turned away from a rule and legacy of wickedness and pain to look into the future with hope. The prospect of new beginnings rested on the shoulders of a seven-year-old ruler named King Joash.

You can almost visualize the moment when Athaliah, the mother of the dead wicked king Ahaziah, saw commotion at the temple. Hearing all the noise, celebration, and declaration, she went to the temple to see what was going on. To her bitter spirit, it wasn't a moment of celebration like the rest but of despair. While gazing at a young boy who now stood in the position that her late son held, she saw the king, standing by the entrance of the historic temple surrounded by biblical Secret Service agents and rejoicing. Loud trumpet blast along with singers and other musical instruments were the declaring orchestra that would partake of this memory leading the praise and worship. Locals celebrating hope as they embraced the moment. However, the broken and destructive mother Athaliah tore her robes and blustered, "Treason! Treason." Priest Jehoiada with the vision to protect and pave a way for King Joash sent hundreds of soldiers to capture her.

2 Chronicles 23:14–15

[14] ... "Bring her out between the ranks and put to the sword anyone who follows her." For the priest had said, "Do not put her to death at the temple of the Lord." [15] So they seized her as she reached the entrance

of the Horse Gate on the palace grounds, and there they put her to death.

The legacy of an iniquitous generation was ended freeing the oppressed. Priest Jehoiada made a covenant and promise to live and follow the Lord's commands; a vow that the king's people and he himself would all be the "Lord's people." With this charge, the next step that was taken was to remove the place of idol worship. They went into the temple of Baal and destroyed it. Breaking down the altars, they got rid of the idols and killed the priest of the false god Baal also named Mattan. These men of God were literally cleaning house and removing anything that was against the commitment and covenant they made with God to be the Lord's People. Jehoiada still delegating and placing trusted people in ranking positions, commissioned Levities once again to manage the temple. With hundreds of warriors and other noble people of power and laymen alike, they marched into the palace and sat the king at his rightful place. There sat a seven-year-old ruler under the counsel of a priest who deeply cared. Jehoiada provided leadership that cared enough to remove hindrances and destructive voices and dispatching idols and other forms and influences of false worship. Many people moved and acted, so King Joash could start his reign free of the obstacles that could get in the way of the God covenant and standards he was committed to.

2 Chronicles 24

Joash Repairs the temple

24 "Joash was seven years old when he became king, and he reigned in Jerusalem forty years. His mother's name was Zibiah; she was from Beersheba. ²Joash did what was right in the eyes of the Lord all the years of Jehoiada the priest. ³Jehoiada chose two wives for him, and he had sons and daughters.

King Joash was at the tender age of seven years old when he took the great responsibility of becoming king. For forty years, he sat in the throne of kingship and ruled. He started leading well as the Word of God states: he was "right in the eyes of the LORD." One very important reality that King Joash had, which could be accredited toward his success in leading in a Godly manner, was that in his primary years, he had Godly counsel. Not only did he have Godly counsel available to him, but he listened to it. A priest named Jehoiada played a central role in King Joash's life as he instructed him and gave him guidance. We all need healthy Christ-centered voices in our lives to help guide and lead us in the path God has for us. We need people in our lives who can encourage us when we feel down—individuals who will push us toward our God given purpose when we want to quit. Mentors that will correct us if we are walking down a wrong path.

Proverbs 15:22

22 "Plans fail for lack of counsel, but with many advisers they succeed."

The first great exploit that King Joash put his attention toward was rebuilding the temple that gave him refuge at the infancy of his life. To achieve this immense undertaking, King Joash required funds and material. The young king reinstituted a tax that Moses set in place years ago. Due to the destruction and desecration of the temple during the leadership of Athaliah sons, a new chest was made to collect the funds. Her sons trespassed into the temple and took items consecrated for Godly use and exploited them for worshiping the idol god Baal. After coming out of years of oppression and living in a season of new beginnings, the people gladly sowed into the rebuilding of the temple. King Joash's task was greatly received and celebrated. Due to King Joash's leadership and the other voices of wise counsel around him, they had a consistent stream of income pouring in to achieve the task at hand. The funds were used to hire masons, carpenters, blacksmiths, and others skilled and honored with the assignment of the renewal and renovation of the temple. They rebuilt the temple not only to the original blueprint God required, but also reinforced it.

It is certain that people were already rejoicing and talking well of the young king and what he was doing for God. He was fulfilling his duties of the crown, upholding the standards he was anointed with and vowed to keep. Once the temple was finished, the money was brought to Priest Jehoiada, father figure and mentor to the king. He along with the king invested the funds to create articles to be used in the temple. All of this started because of one who chose not to sit down and do nothing. Jehoiada was a priest who said to himself, enough is enough. He was a man of God who showed his strength and assembled hundreds of commanders to liberate nation from oppression. Jehoiada was a pillar of wisdom and an example to King Joash, and he vowed his service to the Lord and to the king. However, just like all people living today, our life has an expiration date, a day and time that is unknown to us, yet we are aware it is coming. Jehoiada died at the old age of a hundred and thirty years old. The honor that was bestowed on him was remarkable as he was buried with the kings in the City of David. Why? Because of all the astounding, accomplishments he attained in his life. He would sure be a voice that would have been missed, a voice of counsel that King Joash would soon disregard.

The Downward Slope

2 Chronicles 24:17–18

The Wickedness of Joash

"17 After the death of Jehoiada, the officials of Judah came and paid homage to the king, and he listened to them. 18 They abandoned the temple of the Lord, the God of their ancestors, and worshiped Asherah poles and idols. Because of their guilt, God's anger came on Judah and Jerusalem."

Once the late priest Jehoiada passed, the culture experienced a harsh shift in morals. The work that Jehoiada worked so hard to oversee and cast vision for was quickly cast aside as if it were no longer needed.

King Joash along with many others abandoned the temple. They abandoned the temple that the king cast vision to build, the temple that King Joash gave motion to, to raise money for, so it could be restored. Not only did they abandoned the temple, but they started to worship false idols and Asherah poles. Asherah poles were statues built and raised up to worship mother goddess Asherah. This idol and false god was considered a fertility god. Once the standard that reinforced God-founded ideologies were removed from the king's life, he turned his back on the Lord. Why would the king spend all the time, money, and effort to rebuild a temple that he would neglect and reject later in life? Why did he shun the very building project that had marked his legacy the moment that his mentor and father figure passed away? Maybe it was because he only did it for Priest Jehoiada. Did he do it simply to appease the priest and those around him? Was the conviction of the Lord and the mission to restore the temple ever his own? Did he restore the temple because it was part of the burden of the crown, or was he just chasing after a trophy? King Joash tossed away the covenant and promise he made when crowned king. He disregarded the commitment he made to God and the people. Was the building of the temple just a trophy for him, so he could look back at his life and say, "Look what I have done"? Was the temple simply a sample of his own achievements? Was he chasing the affirmation and feeling of solely completing a task? Was having a place of worship the paramount aspiration he acquired through the guidance of Jehoiada? King Joash was raised in "church" and not by a father but by a man of God. Were the standards never his own? Was it just the convictions of a one-hundred, thirty-year-old man whom he wanted to appease?

Growing Up in Church

I grew up in church, and though I wasn't thankful for it back then, I am grateful today. I am thankful that my mom and dad would drag us to church every Sunday morning. My dad played in bands growing up, and even though we would leave on the weekends, he would always be back for church. I attended a small country church in Eden, North Carolina. We attended church at 9 a.m. and didn't leave until

1:15 p.m. I felt like King Joash living in the temple of God. Nevertheless, even though I was there all those years, I rejected the word of God and the standards it communicates, even though I never lived out the practices of a Christian I knew how to play church. I knew how to perform even though I ignored the instructions on how to live. I knew when to shout and when to dance but did not care to walk out the Christian responsibilities. I was a Christian in title but not in deed, I was never a Christian at all. All I had was a nametag but never walked in its office. Yes, I knew the motions but ignored the canons. The word of God and pleasing Jesus carried no weight as I thought being in the temple was good enough. Jesus sets clear benchmarks for the expectations He has for every person who wants to be a follower of Christ. "Then he said to them all: "Whoever wants to be my disciple must deny themselves and take up their cross daily and follow me." Luke 9:23

Jesus uses the word disciple to describe the place of commitment required. It's more than just being a follower or a fan but someone who desires to sit under the stewardship of His ministry. People must understand that with this honor comes teaching, correction, encouragement, and other challenging but life-changing experiences.

> The grace of God was never the eraser that removes His standards but a highlighter that makes us aware of the strength He has given us to walk it out.

However, to sit under Jesus Christ's leadership and follow Him has a prerequisite. The requirement is that we must deny ourselves and take up our cross daily. This is the daily engagement of challenging the appetite of our flesh for ungodly nutrition, by starving its defiant pressures our sinful nature pleads to have satiated. Jesus gave clear expectations and still desires them today. The grace of God was never the eraser that removes His standards but a highlighter that makes us aware of the strength He has given us to walk it out.

There must come a place in every believer's life when one puts the flesh to death daily and feeds there spirit. If we are not careful, we can celebrate the trophies and achievements of church services all the while ignoring the character that needs to be adjusted as a culture that thinks that talent takes the place of the anointing and maintaining an idea that preaching well is the same as living well. Trophies that are for our own personal gain will tarnish, but the crown that we are fighting to uphold will have eternal value. Crowns are greater than trophies. Crowns are for Jesus, but trophies are for us. We need to be living our life so that one day, we can lay our crown at His feet, submitting to the dominion that we as kings or queens are over, and called to steward our lives over to the King of kings. Attending a church or just carrying the torch of your family's faith doesn't cause an osmosis of the benefits. It doesn't make you saved; it doesn't give you a VIP pass into heaven that when you die you can say, "Hey, I am with them." Your faith must be owned and lived out by you and you alone. It's this notion that King Joash failed to do. This atrocious act would cost him everything including his very life.

Matthew 7:23

²³ Then I will tell them plainly, 'I never knew you. Away from me, you evildoers!'

The Beginning of the End

2 Chronicles 24:19–20

¹⁹ Although the Lord sent prophets to the people to bring them back to him, and though they testified against them, they would not listen.

²⁰ Then the Spirit of God came on Zechariah son of Jehoiada the priest. He stood before the people and said, "This is what God says: 'Why do you disobey the Lord's commands? You will not prosper. Because you have forsaken the Lord, he has forsaken you.

King Joash was setting himself up for destruction. His appalling actions would cost him greatly. However, God stretched out his arm with the heart to reach out, but Joash slapped his hands away. He rejected the prophets who were dispatched by the Lord. He didn't want anything to do with the Lord and the very truths that helped positioned him in the place of power that he currently resided in. It was as if he believed he alone got himself there by disregarding the hand of God who guided his life though Priest Jehoiada. He snubbed against the idea of going back and would not listen. Even his mentor's son Prophet Zechariah approached him with the vision to see the repentance and transformation needed in him. He told him that he would not prosper any more, but he has turned his back on God anyway. The boldness that the prophet of God would have to say such a thing! To the king, the temple was just another achievement and not a place of worship. It was just another trophy that was gained through his admiration and vision. Who is this son of Jehoiada to tell me such a thing, Joash may have wondered. Zechariah, a son that was present during King Joash crowning, saw when he was handed a copy of the covenant that so many fought, bled, and died for, yet it was so easily cast aside. In King Joash's hardened heart boiled an anger and a dire goal to rid himself of the echo of past standards that Jehoiada raised him in.

2 Chronicles 24:21–22

²¹ But they plotted against him, and by order of the king they stoned him to death in the courtyard of the Lord's temple. ²² King Joash did not remember the kindness Zechariah's father Jehoiada had shown him but killed his son, who said as he lay dying, "May the Lord see this and call you to account."

King Joash had killed the very son of his mentor. How far off in sin and in his own personal gain did he progress that he didn't remember or give attention to the one person who aided him greatly? This act along with the idol worship put the nail in his own coffin. The act of killing the son of a hero who was buried along kings even though he was a priest was the pen that wrote his own obituary. When someone is comfortable with their sin, they will fight, ignore, and kill every voice that lovingly attempts to free them from it. So many well-meaning people who you can call "haters" are the people who love you the most. King Joash not only didn't want to live out truths he was raised under but refused to hear it as well. If we are not careful, we will cast aside the priceless crown we are called to wear for the quest of a corroding trophy. A crown objectifies the servant heart required to lead, whereas a trophy emphasizes our own carnal efforts.

> If we are not careful, we will cast aside the priceless crown we are called to wear for the quest of a corroding trophy

At the start of a new year, an Aram army marched and killed King Joash; thus his reign was over. King Joash was a king who started well but ended tragically, a king who tossed the promises and covenant he made with God for his own personal gain. He had been a man of promise but discarded the teaching that Priest Jehoiada raised him in. King Joash traded all of the great exploits that paved a way for him to be king. He killed the son of his mentor, shaming his name. He was raised in a temple that Athaliah stained with blood, but was the hiding place of an infant with potential to shift the balance of power and influence a body of people. The very temple that many invested time, attention, and funds towards was later omitted from his realm of worthy endeavors. The idols that the legend Jehoiada tore down were built back up by the generation of leadership he was trying to pave a way for. King Joash threw away his crown for trophies.

2 Chronicles 24:25

[25] "When the Arameans withdrew, they left Joash severely wounded. His officials conspired against him for murdering the son of Jehoiada the priest, and they killed him in his bed. So he died and was buried in the City of David, but not in the tombs of the kings."

There lay a dead king in a bed of compromise. Yes, he accomplished great endeavors but at what cost? His name was later written in the book of the kings for rebuilding the temple of God. His achievements were great and valued. Nevertheless, at the end of his life as he lay there, bleeding to death in his own bed, did he ask himself whether the trophies or feats were worth it for the cost of the crown? After he died, the one who took the crown was his son named Amaziah.

Déjà Vu

At the age of twenty-five Amaziah become king of Judah. He grew up seeing the successes and failures of his dad, King Joash. He was a new generation of leadership that could turn the pages of the legacy his father had written. He was given a fresh opportunity to bring the nation back to a state of standards that was vital for them to return to in order to usher convictions that were rooted on God's word and the covenant that was once given. King Amaziah had the chance not to commit the same mistakes his father Joash had done.

2 Chronicles 25:1–2

25 "Amaziah was twenty-five years old when he became king, and he reigned in Jerusalem twenty-nine years. His mother's name was Jehoaddan; she was from Jerusalem. 2 He did what was right in the eyes of the Lord, but not wholeheartedly."

From the very beginning of the word of God's description of King Amaziah life, we read the pivotal breaking point of his life. "He did what was right in the eyes of the LORD, but not wholeheartedly." God doesn't want partial obedience but complete commitment. God disdains lukewarm, double-minded event-based faith that is established in a mindset of carnal and selfish motivation. At the start of his rule, the king "shot himself in the foot." He ruled with a little bit of God and a dash of himself. Verse two of 2 Chronicles 25 foreshadowed the cause of what would one day be his demise.

At the outset of his rule, once his leadership was steadfastly established, he had ordered the death of the officials that slaughtered his father King Joash. He was missional as he gathered up an army of people ready to take up arms and fight. Preparing the stage for great exploits in which his name would be remembered, King Amaziah and his army marched to the Valley of Salt and dismembered and killed ten thousand men of Seir. To add to this horrific battle scene, they apprehended ten thousand additional men alive and threw them over a cliff where they died a gruesome death.

There is no doubt that the king's name may have been voiced with respect due to this military endeavor. A young adult wearing the crown would lead an army to victory. However, in the midst of his monumental moment, he made a choice that would be the "kiss of death" to himself. It was a choice that would sadly continue the pattern of behavior that his father had modeled—a mindset that wasn't confronted but ruled his thought process.

2 Chronicles 25:14–15

[14] "When Amaziah returned from slaughtering the Edomites, he brought back the gods of the people of Seir. He set them up as his own gods, bowed down to them and burned sacrifices to them. [15] The anger of the Lord burned against Amaziah, and he sent a prophet to him, who said, "Why do you consult this people's gods, which could not save their own people from your hand?"

King Amaziah and his divided heart gathered idol gods and started to worship them. He, like his dad, had forsaken the standard that wearing that crown epitomized and chased after trophies and idols birthed out of his own achievements. Crowns are greater than trophies.

In the task of his own goals and achievements, he deserted the Lord and started to worship his own work. Once again, another king who started off well but ended in tragedy. A prophet of God and the voice of reason went to the king to speak truth and to resolve this massive mistake. However, King Amaziah, in the state of his pride and ego, refused to listen to the man of God.

2 Chronicles 25:16

> [16] "While he was still speaking, the king said to him, "Have we appointed you an adviser to the king? Stop! Why be struck down?" So the prophet stopped but said, "I know that God has determined to destroy you, because you have done this and have not listened to my counsel."

Just as in King Joash's situation, God attempted to turn the ship that was leading them downward to their destruction. Nevertheless, the sail of their own willpower was open, allowing the wind of pride to usher them wherever their flesh desired. God offered aid yet, the medications to this ungodly mentality were rejected. They adopted and nurtured the evil choices committed. While the prophet was speaking, he stopped him midsentence and threatened his life. When we are solely chasing a trophy, we become blinded by all voices of reason and truth. God tries to shake us awake to see the dangerous path we tread upon. The king in modern day terminology was asking, "Who are you to tell me what to do?" Who was He? He was the man God sent as an expression of love and desire to see his heart turned back to the Father. He was the billboard, the marketing ploy of God to communicate the father's heart to the declining King Amaziah. If only the king would remember the promise that the crown represented rather than the trophies he was seeking.

King Amaziah went on to fight in a battle that would end up being his last. He rejected the counsel to stay home that his ego was coaching him to ignore. The king of Israel named Jehoash attacked him and captured him. Not only did the king of Israel capture him but he also raided the temple of God who King Joash his father and Priest Jehoiada worked so hard to restore.

2 Chronicles 25:24

[24] "He took all the gold and silver and all the articles found in the temple of God who had been in the care of Obed-Edom, together with the palace treasures and the hostages, and returned to Samaria."

In his condition of disobedience, his legacy was being destroyed. His state of folly in refusing to live for the Lord wholeheartedly had cost him significantly. A tarnishing trophy would once again cost a heavy crown. This transaction of personal gain and entitlement would rob so many of God's blessings and provision.

2 Chronicles 25:27–28

[27] "From the time that Amaziah turned away from following the Lord, they conspired against him in Jerusalem and he fled to Lachish, but they sent men after him to Lachish and killed him there. [28] He was brought back by horse and was buried with his ancestors in the City of Judah."

Its Déjà vu once again, a broken record, or a song on repeat. We read it before, we saw it before, we know the outcome, yet we keep committing the same crime. It is the crime that we treat Jesus as an option and his standards as wishes rather than commands. It is the transgression of God's heart and the infringement toward His great sacrifice on the Cross of Calvary. The danger of half-hearted worship and devotion is unquestionable. Nevertheless, the problem can be mended by true repentance and a lifestyle change.

King Amaziah died just as his father King Joash and his father before him, King Ahaziah. They died repeating the same pattern of behavior. Living with a static mindset that couldn't be altered, they rejected all Godly counsel. They forgot the price of the crown they bore and ignored the promises they made in bearing it. Three generations of leaders ran up against the same obstacle. Following the death of King Amaziah, his son King Uzziah, grandson of King Joash was crowned the king of Judah.

CHAPTER 2
WHOLEHEARTEDLY

We live in a society where it seems that our faith and beliefs are truths that we put on and off when it is convenient, treating the word of God as if it is a buffet picking and choosing what taste good and what isn't appealing to our flesh. We live in dangerous times as many people are adopting a reasoning that the issues that Jesus thought was worth dying for are now worth living out today. We are living in a place in history where we are allowing culture or popularity to create the standard of a Godly lifestyle, all the while we have the Word of God who is written out for us. We have to understand that the word of God wasn't written so we couldn't have a life or live in the joys of life. The word of God and God's standards for our lives are so that we can have a healthy and powerful life. We can no longer live a life where we are compartmentalizing the faith and Christian standards.

A popular television station indirectly communicates the appetite for individuals who don't desire to live out consistent Christianity. Sunday afternoon until Sunday morning the station broadcast ungodly music videos filled with profanity, sexual displays, and other obscenities. The artists there are highlighting the love of money and doing whatever you have to do to get it, endorsing and celebrating how many "side chicks" you have and how unfaithful you can be. Throughout the week, you would think that this station is solely focused on delivering what is popular and desired by the populace, but when Sunday morning arrives, it shows preaching, worship, and Christian music videos. Now don't get me wrong; I think it is awesome that the gospel is being preached, and they're praying that people are being reached. However, the preaching, teaching, worship, and other Godly examples are over once Sunday afternoon arrives. The station is feeding us what it recognizes as the weekly model of the average believer. It says "I can live as if Jesus has no standards for me throughout the week as long as I give him praise on Sunday morning for a few hours, then I am a man of God or a woman of God." That is dangerous thinking and not a lifestyle that Jesus paved a way for us to live, which is wholehearted worship and wholehearted living. Yes, we all make mistakes, yes, we all fall short, but we have a choice to stand and keep walking. To adopt the mindset that our faith and standards can take a break when it is fitting is hazardous. This may not be popular teaching, but it is imperative that we take the reins of our attention and put them back on Jesus so that we are not satisfied with simply attending a church service and thinking that that is good enough for God or that we've completed our weekly duties as Christians.

James 1:22

22 "Do not merely listen to the word, and so deceive yourselves. Do what it says."

A Morbidly Obese Church

I will never forget the open vision I had when I was at my church in Asheboro, North Carolina, called First Assembly of God. There I attended and graduated from the North Carolina Masters Commission, which is a Bible school internship. This movement has aided in training many young people to be ministers of the gospel whether in full-time ministry or in marketplace ministry. One day I was by myself in the sanctuary praying, as all my classmates and peers were out at a restaurant having a great time. More than likely, the fire-filled believers were at a joint called "Cookout" which is heavenly. I didn't go and decided to spend time in prayer, not because I was more spiritual than the rest or antisocial but because I was broke and didn't have money. I would receive no joy watching others take a bite of a mouthwatering, greasy burger while chasing it down with one of the hundreds of flavors of milkshakes Cookout has to offer.

As I was pacing back and forth on the floors of First Assembly seeking the face of God, I had an open vision. I will never forget this moment that marked my life. Even as I close my eyes today, I can vividly recall and see this experience. Knowing that I was alone at the church, crying out to God, I was startled when I saw a morbidly obese woman sitting the very back of the church. I am by no means making fun of weight or attacking the struggles that those who combat obesity face every day. However, in this open vision as the Lord opened my eyes to see what He wanted me to see that day and learn the lesson He was communicating to me, there was no physical way this woman could be alive or even real. She was so large that she took up the entire pew that she was sitting in. I remember seeing her dressed in her Sunday best with perfectly prepared hair. Her makeup looked as if a professional had done it. It was noticeable that she took her time getting ready to go to church. I then noticed that the pew that she was sitting on had broken right down the middle. She had one cheek on the far left of the pew and the other cheek stretched out to the far right. I recall asking God out loud the question as I was discerning that this was a vision, "God, who is that"?

God then told me, "Timothy, that is my church."

I proceeded to ask Him, "God, why is she so big?"

"Timothy, my church has been coming in my house eating and eating of my Word but has not exercised their faith. Because they have not exercised their faith, they have lost their mobility."

I don't believe in knocking down the church or creating a ministry that is preaching against the church. However, I firmly believe that God was giving me a wakeup call and stirring up a passion to actively move the modern-day church to fulfill her purpose today, to share its encounters, and vision that marked me. Now as I travel as an evangelist, it aids in motivating me to help the church to see and exercise the truths we know.

1 Corinthians 4:20

"For the kingdom of God is not a matter of talk but of power."

We can't be a church or Christians that think hearing the message is good enough; we have to carry it out. We must exercise our faith. We must be the hands and feet of Jesus. We are the billboards, the advertising, and the representatives of Jesus Christ here on earth. A Christian without a mission isn't a Christian at all. Make up in your minds to be a mobile follower of Jesus Christ. We can't solely and simply be a library of archived memories of the things and testimonies God used to do or has done for us. We can't be a building of antique people, just holding on to the memory and the value of yesterday's manna. Jesus still desires to move through us just as we read in the book of Acts—and greater. We as the church are like nurses to the "Great Physician." We prepare people to lie on the operating table of Jesus's love and presence. When you walk into the doctor's office, one of the first steps that the nurses or representatives of the practice has you do is to fill out a form. The form is asking you questions about what symptoms you have, and it is expected for you to be honest. If you lie about your problems or are not transparent about what is really going on, if you're dishonest about your issues, then the doctor can't treat your problem, as you are nurturing a lie. The questionnaire also asks you questions about your family history and your past.

Be honest in answering the questions about what struggles and illnesses your parents and your grandparents had or have, so when you see the "Great Physician," He can give you aid in your time of need and equip you to face the circumstances that has been plaguing your past, giving you the chance to break the cycle and create a new standard. Be the one in your family to draw a line in the sand and say enough is enough. Take a stand and say that divorce stops with you, that depression has been served its notice, and it is evicted from your family. All it takes is one person who is sick and tired of being sick and tired to create a standard that breaks a pattern of behavior. Sadly, the three examples of the kings started well, with the goal to be different but ended the same. King Joash, King Amaziah, and King Uzziah, three generations of men who had the chance to end the cycle, failed to do so because they did not wholeheartedly give their lives over to the Lord. King Joash the grandfather, King Amaziah the father, and King Uzziah the son all reigned at different times but, just as the television station, they compartmentalized their faith.

One of the greatest threats against God's purpose for our lives is the mindset of being "good enough," that is, when we have enough of the right things to outweigh the bad, and we maintain a mindset that Jesus will celebrate partial obedience. Why is it that in our faith, we carry this belief, but in everyday life, we know that it won't suffice? Bakers understand that if they are going to bake a cake, then all the ingredients are required with nothing left out. If they gather the butter and the eggs but leave out the flour, then they won't end up with the envisioned or expected product. Why? Because they are missing key components to achieve the desired outcome. They won't have a cake but a mixture of premature batter. The baker can't blame the oven for not being hot enough or blame the eggs for being bad because the fact of the matter is, they are void of ingredients. He needs to follow the process and the recipe wholeheartedly. So many areas in our everyday lives require order and process. It demands complete obedience to the vital steps required, so it can be what it is created to be and what it is was meant to be used for. If we don't live our lives wholeheartedly for Jesus, then we will not produce the fruit we were created to have.

My Mobile Church

One of my first cars was handed down to me from my father. I was around sixteen or seventeen years old, and just like many other teenagers, I was eager to drive. While others in my school were driving more modern cars, I had a "throwback Thursday" type of mode of transportation. My first car was a 1985 Oldsmobile. I remember the first place

I drove the car was to a little church in Eden, North Carolina, called Piney Fork Baptist Church. I sat in the car, leaned the seat back, and drove that "bad boy" like it was the newest and latest car right out of the dealership. However, the problem was, that it wasn't that way at all. The car was filled with problems and issues. My 1985 Oldsmobile was a ghetto ride but took me from point A hopefully to point B. My father and I painted this car with five cans of grey spray paint from Dollar General. It was a nice rusty matt finished that could only be achieve by the old-school ingenuity that my father obtained. The car also had four doors; however, only two of the doors opened. The Oldsmobile had four windows, but only two of those windows rolled down. It was always quite an ordeal when attempting to go through a drive-through window at a fast-food restaurant. This car wasn't much to look at, but it was my mode of transportation and it was given to me. The 1985 "WIP" air conditioner no longer worked thus in the summer months it was mandatory to dress for the occasion. When it was hot, you had to go to one of the two windows and roll them down, and take some clothes off. When it was a cold North Carolina winter, you once again had to move toward the two windows, roll them up, and add more clothes to combat the freezing weather. I had to make sure I didn't touch the passenger-side window because in the bottom right hand corner, we had a screwdriver holding the glass up. This car was the perfect case study for Xzibit to *Pimp My Ride* in the early 2000 television show. Long trips were always a struggle because I didn't have a radio. If I wanted to change the channel, I simply had to start singing a different song. When driving it short distances, it would constantly overheat. I kept water jugs in the trunk to fill up the radiator both on my arrivals and departures. Despite all the issues this automobile had, it was a blessing because it was better than walking.

I have so many memories in this duct-tape-bound vehicle, one being that I drove to my prom dates house in this car. Yes, my *prom* date! I can only imagine the first thoughts my prom date had when she saw me pull up in her driveway. She probably spent hours getting ready that day, going to the salon to get her "hair did" and her "nails done," and picked out the perfect dress for the perfect evening; it was a day that she had been waiting for all year. Constantly peaking though the blinds and curtains to see if I had arrived yet to walk her to her chariot and debark on a lovely evening. There she was waiting for her knight in chocolate armor to arrive. I bet she was surprised when I finally arrived in a car that was overheating and smoking like Snoop Dogg and making more noises than a Las Vegas stomp routine. I was late because on my way to her house, the car overheated, and I had to stop by a gas station and wait for it to cool down, so I could remove the radiator cap to add water. I vividly recall standing in front of the open hood of my ghetto car in an all-white tuxedo staring at my watch. A stranger then pulled up beside me and offered help pouring in the water because they didn't want my tuxedo to get dirty. That my friends, that is called Southern Hospitality. Thankfully, once I arrived at her house, we decided to take a minivan to the dance. Though this car was not the best running or best-looking car, I had many "Jesus moments" in it. It became my moving sanctuary, my hopefully starting Psalm 91 secret place, my throwback prayer closet, and my mobile church. A place of great encounters with Jesus and great life lessons.

Have you ever been so hungry that you felt like your stomach was going to eat itself? Your stomach sounded like the upper room on the day of Pentecost making all sorts of noises. The hunger *was* so bad that you start getting irritable and needed food at that moment. I was at that point and was on a mission to find nourishment. I was leaned back driving my 1985 Oldsmobile, and I was famished when I saw a billboard advertising a chicken restaurant. It was marketing their amazing finger-licking, mouth-watering fried chicken with all the southern comfort food sides you can think of: dirty rice, mashed potatoes, greens beans, corn on the cob and don't forget potato wedges and the glorious mac and cheese while washing it down with the perfect brewed sweet tea poured in a cup with the "good ice." What is good ice? Find your nearest southerner and ask them what "good ice" is. It's the small tic-tac size ice cubes made of blessed water and thankfulness. The moment I saw that billboard my mind and taste buds were already made up, and I didn't want or crave anything else. I wanted what I saw presented and advertised on that billboard. I passed by burger spots, breakfast restaurants, and mom and pop diners. I didn't want anything else but the product that was presented to me on the road. Finally, I pulled into the driveway of the fried chicken joint, excited and starving, on the brink of perceived death but thankful that my hunger is about to be satiated and my need met. I opened one of the two doors that worked, stepped out of the car and speed-walked to the doors. I had a huge smile on my face as I was filled with expectation to receive something that I had been expecting ever since it was presented to me on the road. There I was, standing face to face with the cashier, the one who is set in place to mediate my request to the cook and present to me the promise shown on the road. With a smile on my face, I asked the lady for a number 2 which was two pieces of chicken a side and a drink. However, the next words that came out of this woman's mouth shook me to my core. It caused me to question the entire establishment. She told me that they were all out of chicken. *What! Yes!* All out of chicken. I am now having so many mixed emotions, thoughts of anger, feelings of hunger, and a mindset of disappointment. My mind, heart, and taste buds were fixed on fried chicken and nothing else. I preceded to asked the cashier why are they were out of chicken. She then told me that there was lack of communication or miscommunication with the distributor, so they missed their shipment. The storehouse was never notified that they had a need or that they needed to be refilled and restocked. I left that place disappointed. Why? Because it was advertising a product it was not producing. It was missing a *vital* step, so it could be what it was created to be: a place of nourishment and the means for hunger to be met. Nevertheless, due to its lack of communication with its provider, it was failing to carry out its purpose.

In the midst of the hardship, God spoke to me and asked me this question. "Timothy, how many times have people come to your restaurant but left disappointed and malnourished because you were advising a product that you were not producing because of your lack of communication with your storehouse, distributor, and provider?" When we fail to treat our relationship with the Lord in a wholehearted manner, we nullify the opportunity to be effective Christians that produce fruit. Sometimes the struggle that society has with Jesus is not that they don't believe that He exists or was once real, but it's that they don't know He is relevant or real today. Why? Maybe because the world has attempted to drive through our lives, churches, and homes only to leave disappointed because we are marketing fruit that we are not producing. It is important to Jesus that we produce fruit.

CHAPTER 3
THE YEAR THAT PRIDE DIED

Three kings, three generations, one crown yet the same

trophy. The legacy of three men who refused to cast aside entitlement, pride, and ego. This grave mistake, which shortened their lives, led to their deaths and shook Judah. The ripple effect of the wave of their actions has echoed through every generation, starting with King Ahaziah. Each king had the chance to end the cycle of idol worship, to halt the pattern of conceded leadership by evaluating the man in the mirror. However, neither made the choice to do so. After chasing a tarnished trophy of popularity and personal gain had taken the life of King Amaziah, his son Uzziah was chosen as king of Judah. Uzziah was made the king of Judah at the adolescent age of sixteen years old.

2 Chronicles 26:4-5

> [4] He did what was right in the eyes of the Lord, just as his father Amaziah had done. [5] He sought God during the days of Zechariah, who instructed him in the fear of God. As long as he sought the Lord, God gave him success.

King Uzziah at his young age, started his reign in a correct manner with a heart that feared the Lord and upheld His commands and statures. Maybe in this time of his life he made a choice to begin a legacy that would be celebrated rather than mourned. He didn't gather idols, and he didn't worship false gods. He sought the Lord, allowing His guidance to aid him in becoming the king he was always intended to be. The danger that he will relentlessly confront is the battle of being consistent. His father Amaziah started out okay as he lived for the Lord but not wholeheartedly. King Uzziah's great-grandfather Joash started noble as long as he had Jehoiada's counsel. However, as soon as Priest Jehoiada died, he tossed aside God and his commands. It was a tangent of atrocious choices that ushered the premature ending of these kings. King Uzziah heeded to Godly instructions as the prophet and son of Jehoiada, Zechariah, had educated him. He'd given him advice and guidance to have reverence for God and live out his commandments. The disparity in King Uzziah, in comparison to the previous kings, was humility. To fear the Lord is not to be afraid of him. It's not the terror that a person can have when they see a snake. It's not the apprehension one adopts when a bad report from the doctor is received. It's not the trepidation acquainted with public speaking or any other experience that demands a state of alarm or anxiety. The fear Zechariah instilled in him was a state of honor and reverence. It's problematic to anyone who doesn't fear the Lord. The adoration of treating God with a heart of honor, and living by His commands rather than calling them negotiable that is the fear we should all carry. We don't follow the Lord with the fear that he is a God sitting on His throne with a belt in one hand and a "chancleta" in the other. We follow the Lord because He loves us and made a way for us to have a relationship with him. In the beginning of King Uzziah's rule, he anchored his leadership on this stable truth. If he kept God as his source, then he was successful. He allowed God's word and covenant to be the measuring stick to what is right and wrong. He did not do as the other kings who used their emotions, feelings, and greed as the compass that directed their decisions.

King Uzziah's exploits were very impressive. He was a man of God with a strategic military mind. Just as the other kings, news of his success quickly spread throughout the land. He battled against the Philistines, the Arabs, and against the Meunites. In his humanitarian act, he rebuilt and restored homes and tombs near Ashdod. His actions seemed to be birthed out of humility and a desire to truly serve his people. As long as his heart was connected to the heart of God, God's heart influenced his hands. The young king's fame quickly spread all the way to Egypt. His actions mustered up thankfulness and gratefulness in the people. The Ammonites gave tribute to Uzziah, and others honored him as well. His father, grandfather, great-grandfather and great-great-grandfather all were gifted in orchestrating building projects. King Uzziah had the towers built and fortified them. Overcoming what seemed to be an impossible task, he built cisterns in the middle of the desert, finding water in the middle of such a dry place to take care of the vast livestock he had. In this exploit to restore and excel, he commissioned people to work in the fields and vineyards in fertile places. King Uzziah's achievements continued and his fame grew even more. He wasn't only preparing the land for harvest but also an army for war. He mustered up hundreds of thousands of men trained for battle. The young king equipped them all with armor and weapons as well as created catapults and large bows connected to the towers he fortified. Truly the "trophies" in and through his life and legacy were great.

His Achilles Heel

The exploits that King Uzziah accomplished were incredible. He carried a vision to restore the land and the people. People knew him by the "trophies" he obtained and celebrated who he was. Alas, as the fathers before him, his life would come to a horrible end. King Uzziah would encounter the sleeper cell assassin that is out on a mission to destroy. This assailant works in the shadows in private, but the effects are seen publicly. Birthed in the heart of unbalanced believers and nurtured via self-praise and accomplishments, He would face an internal battle that would annihilate him externally. This true enemy is named *Pride*. Pride is an enemy that thrives in silence and grows in praise. This terrorist can't be ignored; it must be confronted. The only way to destroy pride is to instigate a confrontation, with humility and brokenness coming to your

> Pride is an enemy that thrives in silence and grows in praise. This terrorist can't be ignored; it must be confronted.

aid. The fires of pride are smothered out by removing the oxygen it needs to breathe, dissolving entitlement, ego, a demanding spirit, and the longing for affirmation no matter the source and cultivating a servant's heart, influenced by the crown we are called to bear, reminding us of the covenant we made with God. Bowing down and placing our crown at the feet of the *King of kings* as pride gasps for its last breath in the heart of a committed believer refusing to share God's glory. Pride isn't murdered; it must be starved. King Uzziah lost sight of the inward monster lurking in his heart that had been passed down from the fathers and generations before him. Little by little as a dog begging for scraps at the master's table, he was slipping pride morsels of glory echoed by the crowned, which was never his to share or to consume. He dined at the table only prepared for one attempting to shove God out of the throne of his heart so pride can uproot itself in its perceived rightful place. Pride whispered enticing words such as "You deserve this" and "You earned this." It manipulated him to think that his trophies give permission even though the crown beckons denial. He partook in glory never meant to be consumed. Just as a meal that doesn't agree with your stomach, he got food poisoning of the heart, but only humility and repentance is the antidote. He bore the same "Achilles heel" that bought down the fathers before him. His was the fault of a spirit of pride invading and being invited into his heart.

2 Chronicles 26:16

[16] *"But after Uzziah became powerful, his pride led to his downfall. He was unfaithful to the Lord his God, and entered the temple of the Lord to burn incense on the altar of incense."*

There is nothing wrong with achievements and reaching goals. There isn't fault in feats of grander accomplishments. The ambitions, which King Uzziah carried within, benefited countless people. His aspirations to aid in the restoration of Judah were noble as he sought the Lord and obeyed His standards. The shift happened when King Uzziah allowed the praise of people to get into his heart. The compliments about how great he is may have befuddled him from his Godly path. Maybe, it didn't happen in a day; maybe he stood strong for a long time, but when you let your guard down, our sinful nature attempts to take over. When the young king first started, the weight of the crown and what it represented was a reminder of the God he served and why he served the people. The rebuilds and other tasks were fruits from a servant's heart connected to the heart of God, not that of a self-involved king who used achievements as a measuring stick for his own ego. There isn't an error in being rich, popular, and successful. The blunder occurs when we lose our heart for the sake of carnal and earthy things. Once again as his fathers and generations before him, they allowed success to rust away the crown they wore and chased tarnishing trophies. His current diagnosis for pride was shown by his life-changing choice in the temple.

Burning incense in the altar of incense was a task that was never given nor presented to King Uzziah. This undertaking was given to the Levites and the priest. However, for whatever reason, the lost king took it upon himself that the standards didn't apply to him. Azariah and eighty other priests challenged King Uzziah in the error of ministering in the temple. They went into the temple to confront King Uzziah with a mission in which the priest during King Amaziah's reign had also. The priest told the king to leave the sanctuary for he was unfaithful and dishonored the Lord by his actions that he didn't think were a big deal but would cost him greatly. Raging while handling a consecrated article of worship in his hand, he began to argue with the men of God. In the lowest point of his life was the pinnacle of his pride, he could no longer walk that tight rope with unbalanced convictions and fell to his own demise.

> In the lowest point of his life was the pinnacle of his pride, he could no longer walk that tight rope with unbalanced convictions and fell to his own demise.

In the moment, when true repentance could have shifted everything, his ego became earmuffs that refused any advice or instructions to change. He was in a time that he needed to remember what the crown on his head represented. Nevertheless, instead of dropping the censer, listening to the priest, he began to argue with the priest. What could the exchange of his passionate words entail? What was the point that he was trying to get across in that moment of compromise. Could it be words like "Do you know who I am"? Maybe it was statements, such as "Who are you to tell me what to do"? Or maybe it was, "My family built this temple; if it wasn't for them no one would have it." Did he feel entitled to it? Why did he do it? "Only God can judge me"? This king was carrying over the same cycle that the father before him had when King Amaziah stopped the prophet mid-sentence when he compelled him to repent. Snubbing the chance to change and leave, a disease that eats away flesh called leprosy broke out on his forehead. Just like pride, it starts out at a small location but quickly spreads to effect other areas of one's life. Sadly, it took this shocking act to gain King Uzziah's attention, and he was quickly escorted out of the temple. The fact worth noting is that the priests confronted the king out of concern for him. They knew that you don't mess around with the presence and standards of God. For King Uzziah, it was a gradual compromise that had death waiting at the end of the journey.

Gradual Compromise

King Uzziah was confronted at the "altar of incense." He wasn't at the entrance of the temple but in the holy place. Whatever motivated his actions blinded him all the way down to his death. He stepped through the eastern entrance into the "courtyard." He was one curtain away from the Holy of Holies where he would have died instantly. The fact that the priest confronted him wasn't solely out of duty but, I believe, out of concern. Regrettably, gradual compromise was a plague that festered in the heart and mind of the king and the kings before him. The endangerment of pride's selfish counsel is that it cares not for your spiritual wellbeing but your carnal appetite to indulge whatever the source. King Uzziah started well, but along the way he lost sight of the race he was running. As in running track, you must keep your eyes focused and your mind alert. While running you shouldn't look beside you or behind you because you will step out of your lane and become disqualified. Your shoulders become a rudder of a boat and steers you in the direction of your distraction. Along the journey of a king with great potential and renowned exploits, he got distracted and veered off course.

Walk, Stand, Sit

Psalm 1

"¹ Blessed is the one
   who does not walk in step with the wicked
   or stand in the way that sinners take
   or sit in the company of mockers,
² but whose delight is in the law of the Lord,
   and who meditates on his law day and night.
³ That person is like a tree planted by
   streams of water,
   which yields its fruit in season
   and whose leaf does not wither—
   whatever they do prospers.
⁴ Not so the wicked!
   They are like chaff
   that the wind blows away.
⁵ Therefore the wicked will not stand in
   the judgment,
   nor sinners in the assembly of the righteous.
⁶ For the Lord watches over the way of the
   righteous,
   but the way of the wicked leads to destruction."

Psalm 1:1 starts off by revealing the steps required to have a blessed life. The blessing comes when we are positioned to receive it. It is poured out when a person prepares themselves by choosing to abstain from sinful acts. Many desire to be blessed but refuse to take the mandatory steps to obtain it. Walk, stand, and sit is a progression of compromise. When temptation comes in our lives, we need to walk by it and not entertain it. Refuse to have a conversation with the addiction that may entice you to stay.

Proverbs 4:14–15

[14] Do not set foot on the path of the wicked
   or walk in the way of evildoers.
[15] Avoid it, do not travel on it;
   turn from it and go on your way

This is the easiest moment to say no. Why? Because it hasn't been tasted yet. When we walk in the mall and make the journey to the food court, there are often representatives of a restaurant offering samples. They aren't presenting that choice morsel of perfectly prepared sesame seed chicken to you because they are trying to feed you. It's not like the average southern bell, Mason jar sweet tea-drinking momma who offers to feed everyone who steps foot in her house. You don't see the workers wearing their aprons with a toothpick, showcasing a sample of food saying, "You hungry baby? Let Momma fix you up something right quick!" Not at all, the representatives of that establishment are waving the sample in front of you, hoping that if you eat it, it will spark an appetite from more. It is at this moment that it is the easiest stage to smile, say no thank you, and keep walking away, which is the character used to demonstrate the process of a blessed life refrained from giving into the temptation of the progression of compromise. So if you find yourself in a situation of temptation, learn from *Finding Nemo* and just keep swimming. Don't take the bait, believing that your flesh is trying to aid you. Next thing you know you will be battered with eggs and flour and deep-fried. If we give into the lustful desires of our flesh, we aren't fulfilling the blueprint of a blessed life. Walk, stand and sit are three actions that are progressive compromises. It's easy to walk past, but if we are enticed by what is being presented or offered, we could stand in the moment curious about the product or situation. Standing and listening to the salesman offer an item that you assume will make your life better or easier, you purchased items such as those being offered, but they are now in a box in your garage to sell at a yard sale. The blessed man didn't entertain the sinners around him by standing with them in their company. Last, the blessed man didn't "sit in the seat of mockers." The developing steps of compromise will end in sitting, joining, and partaking in the same conversations and actions that were supposed to be walked past. At this point, you ate the sample, stood in line, and swiped your debit card. You paid a price to sit and eat what was offered to you. Obviously, there isn't anything wrong with eating at the mall, but sin in our life is offered in the same way. *First sin is presented, then it is pondered, and finally it is pounced upon.* We will walk in a blessed life if we can continually keep in mind the red flags of those three "P's": Presented, Pondered, and Pounced.

> First sin is presented, then it is pondered, and finally it is pounced upon.

It is *presented* when it is offered or appears and *pondered* when you judge the pros and cons of partaking, weighing out your options and contemplating the concession and derogation of your moral compass. *Pounced* is when you acted on the choice to commit the act of treason against the values and code of conduct of God's word. Even an educated response or a fleshly impulse or reaction, the fruit is still the same. The invitation of sin and its crazy cousins will always bring drama and won't know when to leave. Sin doesn't take the hint that it has overstayed its deceitful welcome; it must be forced out.

Psalm 1:2 discloses the inward drive that the man had, which fueled him to disregard the pressures that fall around him. He put value in the word of God and pondered on it day and night. How is it possible to be in the word all day? Does it mean that for me to live a blessed life that I should spend all my waking hours in my prayer closet? No. We can meditate on His word all day by hiding the scriptures in our hearts. When we memorize the word of God, we have access to it all of the day. A wellspring of hope and reminder of God and His promises. A treasure chest that once opened, enriches the heart of the reader.

The blueprint of a successful and fruitful life is found right here in scripture. King Uzziah at the infancy of his reign applied these truths.

However, just as the kings before him, he would start off well but end horribly. When we lose sight of who we are serving, we create an understanding that we are serving ourselves. *The crown was never meant to be a symbol of the greatest leader but of the greatest servant.* A constant reminder of leading in humility to better the people under your stewardship. The heavy crown was an inherited obligation that the fathers before him should have shown him how to bear.

It was the festering open wound of pride that was toxic to the life of King Uzziah. The rust of his crown happened as he polished his trophies. His Godly standards were ignored but his deeds celebrated. The writer of 2 Chronicles 26:16 denotes that "his pride led to his downfall." Pride chases glory, longs for attention, and thrives from the accolades of others. In the hub of that tornado of inward destruction is an ego that consistently needs affirmation. A tapeworm eats the nourishment from the host; thus it keeps the person always wanting more no matter the source or cost. King Uzziah hosted a parasite that aided in his downfall.

If you long to see the glory of God in your life, the first thing that must be put to death is pride. In the book of Isaiah, chapter six, begins a commissioning moment for the prophet Isaiah. The writer marks that moment in time as the year that King Uzziah died. "In the year that King Uzziah died, I saw the Lord, high and exalted, seated on a throne; and the train of his robe filled the temple." Isaiah 6:1

"In the year that King Uzziah died." What led to his death? His pride. You could read Isaiah 6 like this, "In the year that (*Pride*) died, I saw the Lord, high and exalted, seated on a throne; and the train of his robe filled the temple." When our pride is put to death, we give God greater access into our life. We have the honor to see His glory flow through us in great measures. *But*, first pride must be dethroned. When King Uzziah sat on the throne when he was first crowned, God sat in the throne of his heart. However, as time went on, God was removed and replaced. If you want more of God, there must be less of you. His crown should be greater than our trophies.

CHAPTER 4
A TARNISHING TROPHY

Every one of us should have a desire to be successful, and a heart to achieve and reach our dreams. We should cultivate a heart that is eager to chase toward our God-given purpose. There isn't anything wrong with wanting to win. Nevertheless, the error is welcomed when we choose to win or gain at any cost. If you have to sacrifice your family for a larger ministry, then that isn't winning. If you have to go on illegal drugs to get you above the rest, is that really winning? For some, they must win not matter what. This is the inherent danger of having a mindset that is solely chasing trophies. Yes, we will win at the end, but who is going to be at the finish line with you? How many broken relationships are you going to have to step over? How many missed commitments or shattered promises were used as currency to obtain that tarnished trophy? Again, winning in itself is something to be celebrated, but the journey is what needs attention. Oftentimes when all we can see is the prize at the end of the tunnel, we bypass the life along the way. Everyone and everything else becomes collateral damage or a nuisance. We will miss our children's football games, family events, and other foundational moments in an adolescent life. Don't get me wrong; life happens for all of us: work schedules can be crazy, and sometimes you can't help but miss a few dates along the way. However, the child trying to get your attention at night as you are attempting to prepare for the assignment at work week after week and year after year, may grow up thinking that your trophy is more important than the crown you wear as a parent.

The drive to be successful and obtain what we desire in life is a consent battle of balance between work and family. If you have a nagging thought that this truth might only be for the 9-to-5 working individual in your relationship, then think again. Could you be using your house as your trophy? A home attained through hard work and years of saving as the stubbing block or excuse may cause a wedge in your relationship. Are you always cleaning at the times that you could be playing and making memories? Are you pastoring at the dinner table and fighting monsters in your children's closet, so they can sleep at night? Or are you always stressed, yelling, or frustrated because of the mess that is in your house? Are you so overwhelmed by the task that you forfeit your relationships in your home? This is the real battle every one of us faces every day. How do I stay faithful as well as successful? The necessities of life can't be overlooked. We need a home to live in and funds to live on. Martha felt the same way when Jesus visited her home in Luke 10:38–42

At the Home of Martha and Mary

[38] As Jesus and his disciples were on their way, he came to a village where a woman named Martha opened her home to him. [39] She had a sister called Mary, who sat at the Lord's feet listening to what he said. [40] But Martha was distracted by all the preparations that had to be made. She came to him and asked, "Lord, don't you care that my sister has left me to do the work by myself? Tell her to help me!"

[41] "Martha, Martha," the Lord answered, "you are worried and upset about many things, [42] but few things are needed—or indeed only one. Mary has chosen what is better, and it will not be taken away from her."

Martha, a woman of great intentions and in an honorable deed, invited Jesus and His disciples over to her home. Jesus and at least twelve other hungry men were welcomed and fellowshipped in her place of residence. I can only imagine all the running around she may have been doing, getting cups of water ready for maybe thirteen men after a time of traveling and possibly buckets of water, so they can wash their feet, as it was there custom. The Bible doesn't mention in that passage of scripture that she had servants or anyone else to aid in the house. The only other person the Bible mentioned at that time was her sister Mary. Work had to be done, a job had to be completed, and Martha knew that. This hard-working woman, Martha, was frantically running, trying to get all the needed tasks done to serve Jesus and the other men of God. It wasn't just any other guest; it was Jesus, and everything had to be perfect. As it is in our lives today, it seems like you get your best cleaning done fifteen minutes before company comes over. Your mom is yelling from the kitchen for you to grab the bathroom cleaner and clean the guest bathroom, taking the magazines and other items off the coffee table, turning on candles all around the house, and adding music to set a peaceful ambiance. I can imagine that Mary was telling herself and those around her that the house had to be perfect! Jesus is coming over. Jesus the one who turned water into wine. He is the Son of God who raised the dead and restored the sight of the blind, the man of God who walks on water and fed thousands with five loaves of bread and two fish. He wasn't just anybody; he was "somebody." Anxiously scurrying around the house crossing every "T" and dotting every "I," she didn't want Jesus to visit her mess but rather, dwell in her best.

The Closet of Death

Maybe Mary didn't want Jesus to see her dirt and the things swept under the rug or the closet of death. What is the closet of death? It's the place that one will store all their junk, the items that don't have a place; the closet is typically packed to the very brim and seems if you open the door, everything will fall on you. The closet of death is where you store all the junk in your life, the issues, and problems that have been ignored rather than confronted. There were skeletons that were in the closet. What is in your closet? What problematic encounters in your life have you compartmentalized and placed in a closet of forgetfulness? A great danger is a misleading thought of believing that ignoring the predicament will make it go away. Conversely, the crisis doesn't go away with time, but the wound festers. It isn't biodegradable, and with time, it grows. The only aspect that goes away with time is the opportunity to confront, overcome, and fix the dilemma. Whether covered in dust, the obstacle is still there.

Work had to be done, tasks had to be completed, and chores may have been unchecked. The fact is that there is a predicament that Martha was facing. Martha's sister, Mary, was sitting at the feet of Jesus, hearing his life-changing words, staring at the Lord with eyes in awe while Martha was glaring at her sister with a heart of frustration. The inward struggle and outward actions displayed a feeling that she was abandoned to do all the work by herself. Once again, scripture shows us the constant battle of doing the work that needs to be done while cultivating a relationship for the one whom you are serving. Two woman had two different priorities. One sister saw the task, and the other saw the opportunity. Verse 40 states that Martha was *"distracted by all the preparations that had to be made."* What was she distracted from? She had to work. She was distracted because she put her task above her opportunity to be with and hear from Jesus. The trophy must be reached for, but you can't forget for whom you are running the race. Martha was only offering Jesus her hands, but He also wanted her heart. In a state of frustration and in a straight-forward attitude, she asked the Lord to tell her sister to help with all the work. Now, we all know that the work is important. Without the work being done, no one would eat, and the place would be a mess. In Martha's defense, she thought Mary was in error and that she was right. How many times in your childhood did your parents tell all your siblings to wash dishes or do chores, but someone refuses to lift a hand? You would yell in that cracking voice, "Mom, John isn't helping." You were yelling with the hopes that the authority would put John in his proper place and grab the drying towel to aid in the dishes. Martha assumed the same thing as she told, not asked, Jesus to send Mary to help her. Martha was mad, upset, perhaps yelling, and nagging at Jesus. Imagine sitting around the living room with Jesus. At least fourteen people were chatting, and here comes a distressed, tired, overwhelmed person yelling at the people she is supposed to be serving. One hand on her hip, neck moving side to side like a bobble doll, and snapping her finger in the air outlining a "Z." She went from inviting Jesus to her home to being so overwhelmed by the task to work that she was rude to her company and the ones she was called to serve. Jesus addresses her and tells her, *"You are worried and upset about many things, but only one thing is needed. Mary has chosen what is better, and it will not be taken away from her."* This must not have been the answer Martha was expecting to hear, but it shares a great standard with us. Mary chose to hear what Jesus had to say while Martha was serving; understand the assumption of what was needed. Mary was giving Jesus her heart, but Martha was only giving Jesus her hands.

We must be people who have Mary hearts but also Martha hands. Both are vital in our Christian walk, but it is a slippery slope when you are serving someone who you aren't spending the time to know. So many people in ministry today have found themselves in Martha's shoes, burned out by the load of work so that you start seeing the people you are called to serve as inconveniences and

> We must be people who have Mary hearts but also Martha hands.

weights rather than opportunities. Having and going to church without a relationship with Jesus are actions committed every week around the world. The misleading danger is that "my works for Jesus is same thing as my heart for Jesus." *Our trophies will never take place of our crowns because crowns are greater than trophies.* One day we will pass away and will have the honor to lay our crowns at his feet. The crown that symbolizes our heart to serve Jesus and complete the assignment He gave us. In life, we will receive trophies, but after this life, we will have a chance to give Him our crown. Preach, lead children ministry, set up chairs, go on mission trips, and serve the Lord. *But while serving His name, don't neglect to spend time with His heart.* Many people quit the ministry every day for many reasons. However, for some, it is that they spent more time on the mission than they did with the General of the faith who called them in the first place. It is a scary place in a preacher's and or pastor's life when they open their

Bible for sermon preparation but not for life maintenance. It is paramount that we make seeking and knowing the heart of God a priority in our lives. This life-changing endeavor will affect everything you put your heart and mind to do. *"But seek first his kingdom and his righteousness, and all these things will be given to you as well."* Matthew 6:33

GIVE IT TO ME

We tend to forget what we have because we only see what we want. A great example of this is found in the story of Luke 15.

Luke 15:11–32

The Parable of the Lost Son

[11] "Jesus continued: "There was a man who had two sons. [12] The younger one said to his father, 'Father, give me my share of the estate.' So he divided his property between them.
    [13] "Not long after that, the younger son got together all he had, set off for a distant country and there squandered his wealth in wild living. [14] After he had spent everything, there was a severe famine in that whole country, and he began to be in need. [15] So he went and hired himself out to a citizen of that country, who sent him to his fields to feed pigs. [16] He longed to fill his stomach with the pods that the pigs were eating, but no one gave him anything.
    [17] "When he came to his senses, he said, 'How many of my father's hired servants have food to spare, and here I am starving to death! [18] I will set out and go back to my father and say to him: Father, I have sinned against heaven and against you. [19] I am no longer worthy to be called your son; make me like one of your hired servants.' [20] So he got up and went to his father.

"But while he was still a long way off, his father saw him and was filled with compassion for him; he ran to his son, threw his arms around him and kissed him. ²¹ "The son said to him, 'Father, I have sinned against heaven and against you. I am no longer worthy to be called your son.' ²² "But the father said to his servants, 'Quick! Bring the best robe and put it on him. Put a ring on his finger and sandals on his feet. ²³ Bring the fattened calf and kill it. Let's have a feast and celebrate. ²⁴ For this son of mine was dead and is alive again; he was lost and is found.' So they began to celebrate.

²⁵ "Meanwhile, the older son was in the field. When he came near the house, he heard music and dancing. ²⁶ So he called one of the servants and asked him what was going on. ²⁷ 'Your brother has come,' he replied, 'and your father has killed the fattened calf because he has him back safe and sound.'

²⁸ "The older brother became angry and refused to go in. So his father went out and pleaded with him. ²⁹ But he answered his father, 'Look! All these years I've been slaving for you and never disobeyed your orders. Yet you never gave me even a young goat so I could celebrate with my friends. ³⁰ But when this son of yours who has squandered your property with prostitutes comes home, you kill the fattened calf for him!'

³¹ "'My son,' the father said, 'you are always with me, and everything I have is yours. ³² But we had to celebrate and be glad, because this brother of yours was dead and is alive again; he was lost and is found.'"

In a tale of a two brothers with two different outlooks on their life and situation, Jesus leads this parable talking about the youngest son who is plagued with a desire to get out of his father's stewardship and covering, a son who made the naïve assumption that he could do life better or at least by himself. There is emanate tension in this illustration Jesus shares as we hear and read the harsh words shared from the youngest son's mouth. Raised by a loving, faithful father, the son had an issue getting along. He told his father, the man who God entrusted him to raise and look after, the man who loved him deeply, "Give me my share of estate," so he divided his property between them. He was asking for this money or inheritance prematurely. Before someone passes away, they create a will. The documentation divulges who will receive their possessions after their passing. For some, it is their car, heirlooms, money, or estate. When the young son was asking for his father's estate prematurely, could he have been wishing the death of his own father? Before he asked such as strong request, I wondered if he pondered the thought of what life would be like after his father is dead. If this story took place today, the demand would have been: "Dad, I hate you. I wish you were dead. Give me my money." Why did this immature son ask for his funds early? Why did he demand what he felt was owed to him. Once again, the danger of entitlement and pride was driving the car of his choices. Maybe he got tired of being told what to do or having to follow rules and regulations set by the authority he was under. So he foolishly considered that he would live an abundant life without the blessings, covering, or lordship of his father. All he saw was a trophy filled with money in which his father was the only one standing in his way.

MOVING OUT

An average hormone-driven, hot pocket–eating teenager may have told themselves that they can do better by themselves. After a loving parent tells them no, these words are often stated, "I can't wait to move out of this house." This statement was hollered after the parent said, with a stern glare and an unsympathetic tone of voice, "As long as you are living under my roof, you are going to do what I say." Parenting is not just a responsibly; it is a calling that oftentimes the ones in your flock may not see. The prodigal son desired to move out from under his father's lordship. When someone lives in an apartment or a rental home, they have to sign a lease agreement and follow the standards of the landlord. The landlord owns that property that you may be residing in, but they own it. They set the rules, they set the standards, and you simply abide by them if you want to live there. If the lease says no pets allowed, then it is a concrete understanding that you can't have a dog, cat, or any other animals. You can argue until you are blue in the face, but the standard was written out for you. If the resident refuses to accept the standards, then they will be evicted if there's a known violation after the lease agreement was signed. The bottom line is, if the resident desires to partake in the benefit and resources the home offers, there are standards to be upheld.

Many young people think that moving out is the best option because some are tired of adhering to the rules, only to find out that they themselves will have to pay for toilet paper and that clothing detergent is very expensive and power doesn't just magically appear in the house. I remember coming home from school one day, and my classmates were bragging about how they got allowance. Allowance was a term I never heard in my house nor ever received. Not that getting an allowance is a bad thing, it was just that my parents didn't have the funds to give any. But what my father did show me was a strong work ethic. One evening when my parents were still married and living in the same house, I asked them for an allowance. I begin to tell them how people in my school were talking about all the money they get and how they can buy this video game and that video game. So, in a spirit of entitlement, I asked, "Where is my allowance?" My dad with his southern accent motioned me to come here with his bending finger. As I approached, he then pointed to a light switch that aided in illuminating the room we were having this conversation in. I reached the light switch, and he gave me these simple instructions, which I followed. "Turn the light off" I flipped the switch off and the light left and darkness entered the room. Pausing in a pitch-black room, he then instructed me to turn the light switch back on. I flipped the switch, the lightbulb was then surged with electricity, and suddenly we were standing in a lit room. My father, in a joking yet truthful way, pointed to the lightbulb and said, "There is your allowance." We laughed as a family but I then understood his point. I felt entitled to funds because my peers had them, but by father invested the funds, so at that time in my life, we could have power.

GET RICH OR DIE TRYING

We can't expect all the benefits of living in a leased home but not respect the landlord's standards. For the sake of context, let's call the youngest son John. John, the youngest of two brothers, viewed his situation in an unsatisfied manner. He had a state of mind that he wanted to uproot himself from the lordship of his father. His father, being the landlord of his home, cared for him, but John couldn't see that. John was fueled by an inward drive to chase and claim a trophy of his inheritance at any cost. "Get rich or die trying" is a term that is popular in our generation that encourages a person to chase after the trophy no matter what you lose to get it. John, blinded by his own greed and self-drive, wanted his estate. His father then gave him what he was begging for. John finally got that which he been chasing but would soon find out that he was giving up a lot to gain so little. Not long after he acquired his funds, he packed up all his belongings to get ready to move out of his father's house. He had no vision to move back; he was trying to move forward under a fabricated mindset that the "grass is greener on the other side." If he had a cell phone he might have been calling up his friends about how they are going to party hard. If John had social media, he would have updated his Facebook status, talking about he is finally moving out of his father's house where no one else can tell him what to do. Using hashtags such as #ImGROWN or #SORRYNOTSORRY as trended by so many others that have uprooted themselves from the lordship of their parents. They were eager and excited about what the future held but would soon be surprised when the future opened it hands. John had the resources, but he didn't have maturity. He had the funds, but he didn't have the principles. He obtained a drive but had no clue of the destination that his route in life would take him. He was eager to leave behind his father and his own brother to pursue a tarnishing trophy. His luggage was filled to the brim, and sitting on it was required to zip it up. John took very item that was of worth to him before he took his journey from his home. The Bible tells us that he went to a distant country. He didn't move to be neighbors to his father. He didn't stay in the same city where people might know him and hold him to the same standards that his father did. He moved out to a distant country where no one knew him, a country that didn't adhere to the same Levitical standards that he likely was raised under.

SOURCE AND RESOURCES

John arrived at his destination in the distant country and began to party hard. Maybe he viewed his wealth as an unlimited resource, but it then had a limit. Maybe John was accustomed to going back to his source, that being his father, when he ran out of his allowance and his father would provide him more resources. Being that he willingly left that covering, he also forfeited that benefit. Blinded by fleshly actions and the party lifestyle, he squandered his wealth in wild living. *Wild, being unrestrained, untamed, and making uneducated choices and actions, he discovered his father didn't keep him from living life; his standards protected him so he could have a life.* John was about to see how lonely the finish line is when the race is run only to obtain a trophy because you had to forfeit your team. He spent his money on popping bottles, fake friends, and cheap and or expensive sex with prostitutes. It seemed like he had all the friends in the world when he had the resources, but when that dried up, so did his community. The Bible states that after he spent all his money, a severe famine hit the entire country. Then quickly, he went from buying drinks at the club to off-brand Kool-Aid. He went from eating tomahawk steaks to generic flavored beef ramen noodles. He went from throwing leftovers away to being hungry. It is sad that it took a tragedy to gain his attention, but this started a turning point in his life. He was about to have to face the man in the mirror, step down from his throne of entitlement, and work to live. Now he is working to survive, but when John was with his father, he thrived.

GET A JOB

Just as with anyone who was in a financial dilemma, he went out to look for a job. Before he had servants; now he was looking to serve. Before he had festivals and feasts under the lordship of his father; now he is slaving in the hot sun. He hired himself to a citizen of the region where he tended to the needs of pigs. Imagine the thought that he had when reality hit hard as he was disrobed from his expensive clothing, fancy sandals, and expensive jewelry only to get down in the mud with pigs. John truly walked far from the path he was raised in. John was raised in standards that men of God didn't touch pigs because they were considered unclean. Not only is John touching pigs and other unclean things, but now he is taking care of them. He is getting a harsh awakening that his job now matched his lifestyle. Unclean actions birth other unclean things. He moved out of the home in which his loving father was the landlord, gathered all his wealth, set out to an idolatrous region where his sin would be celebrated rather than confronted. Sweaty, tired, and now hungry, he longs to eat the very slop that the pigs were eating, the leftover of leftovers, the scraps of scraps. As the older generation would say, he "stepped down from his high horse" and was humbled. The next words communicate how fake relationships can be when you have money or somethings to offer verses when you have nothing to give. The Bible states in verse sixteen that "no one gave him anything." They placed more value in the pigs than they did in him. John was now seeing how disregarding the crown to chase a trophy would end up. Was chasing that late-night business deal during your family's Christmas worth your marriage? Was ignoring the tug of your toddler asking you to play with them worth the teen that doesn't even want to be around you? Solely pursing a trophy will usher you down a lonely road that dead-ends in isolation.

Came to His Senses

Finally, John felt the pressure to change outweighed the desire to stay the same. An alteration had to be made, not just in thought, but also in actions. The first conclusion that John arrived at is that he needed to go back to his father. He came to his senses and understood that even the worst day with his father is better than the best day in this season of despair. He came to the understanding that he needed to go back and sit under the lordship of his father. The revelation was that even his father had food to spare and he was starving and longing to dine with the unclean pigs. Being his own cheerleader, he made up his mind that he was going to depart from the road of selfishness and entitlement to go to his father with a repentant and humbled heart.

He Got Up

Step one of his transformation was that he came to his senses. Step two shared in verse twenty is that he got up. *Simply knowing the good you are supposed to do but never doing it will by no means create fruit but excuses.* John could no longer linger in the state of despair and depression; he had to act. He gathered whatever he had left, which assumingly wasn't much, and went back to his father. What transpires next in the word is a powerful illustration of a loving father who is always ready to welcome lost people home. The father looking out of the window of his home toward the end of the road on which his entitled son had departed, a son for whom words couldn't teach but the pain of life would become his mentor. Gazing in the distance, he sees John approaching with a heavy heart and a low-bowed head. The father was waiting for his son, hoping that one day he would coming back under his covering, love, and protection. The patient father saw him while he hadn't yet arrived and was filled with compassion. *I love the fact that we serve a heavenly Father who, even when we haven't arrived yet, is moved at our pursuit toward him.* The father ran toward his son, as if illustrating the profound and powerful scripture in James 4:8 that says, *"Come near to God and he will come near to you."* He embraced John, the younger immature son who earlier wished death upon him. He hugged the son who thought that the trophy that the passion demanded was greater than the community he had under the crown and reign under his father. I can only imagine tears running down John's face as he confessed his mistakes to his father as he shared how imprudent and thoughtless his actions were. In the moment of high emotions and uncovered hearts the fathers actions screamed his love for his son. He motioned to his servant to bring the best robe and place it on him. A ring was given to him, and sandals were placed on his feet. This is what truly happens when a lost person comes back to the father. This is what takes place when we come to Jesus in a true state of repentance. Actions take place in which a great exchange happens where he takes our rags for riches, our depression for peace, our sin for salvation, and our condemnation for redemption. What happened to his robe, sandals, and ring in the first place? Did he take it and pawn it? Did he gamble it away in his selfish living? No matter what happened, he was back with his father. Only His father, the landlord of his home, had the authority to restore his son back to proper standing. This noble transaction ended with John being dressed just as if he never left justified "just as if he never sinned" via way of the works of a loving father. The celebration didn't end there; the father spared no cost as he commanded his servants to kill *the fattened calf* in verse twenty-three. He didn't ask them to kill *a* calf but *the* calf. This is importance because *the* means that it was only one. The father didn't have to explain which calf he was talking about or give further instructions. This calf was set apart for a certain purpose. Whatever the reason may have been, the father had killed "the only begotten calf" to celebrate his son. Why? Because his son was back under his covering, protection, and lordship. Not only was he back, but he was also different. He saw what was at the end of the road of entitlement and came back home humbled. They grilled out and celebrated because of verse twenty-four "For this son of mine was dead and is alive again; he was lost and is found."

Tolerated Rather Than Celebrated

Pride and entitlement is a dangerous duo that will rob blind whoever calls on its destructive aid. Many times people stopped the parable after the youngest son, but the oldest son carried the same problems. For this point, forward let's name the oldest supposedly more mature son Dave. Verse twenty-five starts off the story of the Dave interaction with his father regarding the celebration and homecoming of his younger brother. Dave was in the field working, resting, or just hanging out when he heard music blaring from the house. People in the distance were dancing and in merriment, and Dave wanted to acquire more details so he asked one of the servants what was happening. Words that the servant shared with Dave should have bought a smile to his face, but it was just the opposite. Dave is about to see his selfishness face-to-face as he became angry. The anger was not just pointed toward John, the prodigal younger brother, but also the father rejoicing in his son's saved and transformative return. The servants told him that his brother has come home and that your father has killed "the fattened calf" to celebrate. Dave's selfishness and entitlement reared its ugly head. He threw a temper tantrum and refused to go in the home to party with everyone. Once again, the landlord of the home, his father, came and petitioned with Dave and ask him to come in and rejoice with everyone. The conversation is heated as verse 29 describes the older son expressing his selfish heart and yells, "Look!" At this point, most parents would have grabbed the sandal, wooden spoon, or belt and glared in that young man eyes while grinding teeth with barely moving lips saying, "Who do you think you are yelling at?" Dave begins to pour out his heart and tell his dad that he had been working and done all that was asked of him. He continues tell his father that he never disobeyed an order. He was screaming from a place of entitlement or the notion that he deserved a reward for doing what he was supposed to do in the first place. He says to his father, "You never gave me even a young goat, so I could celebrate with my friends." Hurt people will hurt people, and Dave felt tolerated rather than celebrated. However, he was so selfish all he could think about was himself. He was stuck on focusing on the party and the fattened calf that he cast aside the family he was meant to have fun with. *When you are chasing toward a trophy, you can't rejoice when someone else wins or is celebrated.* Dave continues by belittling his own brother, verbally pushing him down to elevate himself. Verse 30 uses words that are dangerous but many unaware parents use all the time. Words are shared, but to the hearer, communicate disowning or disavowing a person, based upon the approval of actions. He says "But when this *son of yours* . . ."—not my brother but your son, not my blood

> Entitlement becomes blinders that shepherds tunnel vision. It fosters a mindset that negates the peripheral vision of the needs of others because it is fixated on a tarnishing trophy of self-preservation.

but your offspring. The entitlement and selfish exchange with his father simply became a microscope to view in the DNA of this under-cover trophy chaser. He shared with his father all the mistakes that John made and how he killed the calf for him. Entitlement becomes blinders that shepherds tunnel vision. It fosters a mindset that negates the peripheral vision of the needs of others because it is fixated on a tarnishing trophy of self-preservation. The father shared his heart with Dave the oldest son about the benefits of being under the lordship and covering of his home. "My son, the father said you are always with me and everything I have is yours." Truly, the selfishness of the sole desire of the trophy at the finish line with cause you to lose sight of the people you get to do life with in the journey.

John and Dave

Did you find yourself sharing any characteristics with John and Dave? Have you felt like you no longer needed the covering of the Father in your life? One of the greatest mistakes that truly have eternal con-sequences is when we have a foolish notion that Jesus is our Lord *or* Savior not our Lord *and* Savior. We can't have the fruits of the cross all the while neglecting Jesus's leadership in your life. If we want sal-vation, forgiveness, grace, and so forth, then when we must be willing to follow him. Luke 9:23 tells us, "Then he said to them all: "Whoever wants to be my disciple must deny themselves and take up their cross daily and follow me.

Are you taking up your cross and following the path that Jesus has called you to walk? Are you bearing His crown that aids in remem-brance that filters your actions and beckons you to serve? No? Then it's time that you admit yourself in the hospital of His trusted care. Allow His word to be the scalpel that the Great Physician wields to make a heart transplant. He will place you under His care where the anesthesiologist of His presence will put you to rest. He will take out your heart of pride and entitlement and place a heart of a servant and a follower of Christ. I am simply a nurse of the kingdom of God. Before you see the doctor, the questions that this book is asking will aid in prepping you for your appointment. You're in luck because the doctor is available to see you 24 hours a day, 365 days a year. It's time to check yourself in; the doctor is ready to see you.

CHAPTER 5
SEE, SEEK

A terribly misquoted verse is when people say, "Money is the root of all evil." This is simply not true and not what the Bible says at all. Money and funds are needed for everyday life. It is a requisite to aid in the fulfillment of dreams and plans. The same currency that is used at a strip club is the same currency used to build an orphanage. The same "dirty money" can be used to dig wells or send someone on a mission trip. Money isn't the issue; the problem is the source and how the money was acquired. A hundred-dollar bill can't elect whose hands it is in nor can this inanimate object choose evil.

1 Timothy 6:10

"For the love of money is a root of all kinds of evil.
Some people, eager for money, have wandered from
the faith and pierced themselves with many griefs."

First Timothy 6:10 states that the *love* of money is the root of all kinds of evil, not money in and of itself. This is important for many reasons. To start, to blame the money for the actions never gives attention to the holder of the bill. Money is a tool, just as a hammer, a firearm, or a keyboard is a tool. If unsettling activities are done in the pursuit or attainment of money than it is the heart of the holder, not what is in their hands. Secondly, believing that money in itself is inherently evil keeps people poor. Believe me when I tell that that being poor isn't fun. I grew up in great poverty, and we oftentimes lacked money for items such as power and transportation. What we needed was a new mindset, a mindset that would take us out of the cycle of a poverty mindset and into a mindset of believing for funds that would carry us through.

Chasing a Dollar

If, at the end of your journey, life is nothing but a trophy of self-obtainment filled with money but you have no community, peace, or joy at the finish line, is that truly winning? What did that lifestyle cost you? There is nothing wrong with aspiring to be wealthy, drive a nice car, and live in a big house. I pray that you become a multimillionaire and help advance the gospel message all around the world. The quandary occurs when we no longer give attention to the means to reach the end. Have a drive to leave a financial inheritance behind for your family. Work hard to send your children to school. Grind in the office to go on your dream vacation or drive your dream car. Dream big and work hard. Don't chase a dollar; chase after a purpose. *"What good is it for someone to gain the whole world, yet forfeit their soul? Or what can anyone give in exchange for their soul?" Mark 8:36–37*

At the finish line of a race run with selfish intent through the other side of the scarlet ribbon could be isolation and regret. When you look toward the beaten path that was just traversed, what did you miss or misuse to gain that tarnishing trophy? There was a man named Zacchaeus who obtained a lot of money through unethical means. He was a chief tax collector who went through a series of events where he traded his trophies for Jesus's crown.

Luke 19:1–10

"Jesus entered Jericho and was passing through. ² A man was there by the name of Zacchaeus; he was a chief tax collector and was wealthy. ³ He wanted to see who Jesus was, but because he was short he could not see over the crowd.⁴ So he ran ahead and climbed a sycamore-fig tree to see him, since Jesus was coming that way. [5] When Jesus reached the spot, he looked up and said to him, "Zacchaeus, come down immediately. I must stay at your house today." [6] So he came down at once and welcomed him gladly.[7] All the people saw this and began to mutter, "He has gone to be the guest of a sinner." [8] But Zacchaeus stood up and said to the Lord, "Look, Lord! Here and now I give half of my possessions to the poor, and if I have cheated anybody out of anything, I will pay back four times the amount." [9] Jesus said to him, "Today salvation has come to this house, because this man, too, is a son of Abraham. [10] For the Son of Man came to seek and to save the lost."

Richly Poor

Zacchaeus was a chief tax collector. His job was to collect taxes. What caused people to view this man in an unruly manner, was that he was deceitful and a thief. While he was carrying out the duties that his career commanded, he would steal from the people paying their dues. Whatever was required for them to pay, he would add extra and keep the difference himself. His wealth wasn't solely fostered from his typical 9 to 5, but off the backs of faithful citizens. Zacchaeus's actions created an infamous reputation, thus isolating him from community in the process. The cost for his wealth may have been too expensive for him to pay. The weight of debt was due to his choices. When he walked into the room, there would be whispers. Rightly offended people may have huddled together, expressing their concerns but what were they to do? They had to pay taxes, and Zacchaeus just so happened to be the man to take it. All of his wealth came with a great cost. Can you imagine having all the luxury but no one to enjoy it with? Maybe he had a large house but whom would he have over for a meal? Here in the book of Luke is a story about a man hungry for community in a community who wanted him to starve. However, as always, Jesus is the wild card. Our Lord and Savior will always step into the lives of people who birth a desire for him to do so. Even on the way to enter Jericho where Zacchaeus lived, Jesus came across a blind man named Bartimaeus. The blind man was wearing his government-acquired beggar's cloak and was likely overlooked by many, but when he heard that Jesus was passing by he knew that he must seize the moment.

Regardless of what people thought, irrespective of the opinions of man he shouted, "Son of David have mercy on me."

Luke 18:35–43 tells us the story that even those people who lead the way told him to stop, he was yelling to gain Jesus's attention, he was shouting to gain an audience with Jesus. It was after this encounter that Jesus entered Jericho. A moment in time after Jesus just demonstrated that he stops for the desperate, He doesn't overlook the forgotten or the rejected. He refuses to use the same measuring stick that man uses to determine a person's value because He was very aware what they were worth. Why? Because He was about to pay the price on the cross of Calvary. Hearing the faith in the cry of the beggar Jesus sent some men to bring the blind man to Him. Jesus, at that moment, restored the sight of Bartimaeus, and his life was never the same.

Bartimaeus means "son of a noble one, or son of an honorable one." Nevertheless, his handicap robbed him of that position as people only knew him as a beggar. Maybe he became blind later in life and lost everything that his father Timaeus had for him. He went from being rich to poor, but after his encounter with Jesus, he went from poor to rich. His sight didn't have a price tag requiring money to pay, the currency was faith in which he had plenty stored up. When he approached the ATM of the audience with Jesus, he made a withdrawal in which heaven had plenty of resources to cover. Jesus told him in verse 42 of Luke 18, *"Receive your sight; your faith has healed you."* His begging cloak was left on the street corner which used to be his place of residence and now he was following the LORD whom had changed his life. It was after that encounter that they entered Jericho, which they were simply going to pass through. However, faith will always stop Jesus. Others may have thought it was a detour but Jesus viewed it as a pit stop.

See and Seek

Jesus entered Jericho, and as always, He drew a crowd. Imagine, as people are in the marketplace carrying out everyday tasks, buying food for dinner for their family of four that evening, people laughing in the corner stores as familiar customers carry out daily transactions with dry jokes, and couples sitting at the coffee shop dreaming about their future; imagine all of this life is happening in the booming and growing city of Jericho, when all of a sudden the people hear that Jesus is there. Perhaps many never met Him, but likely most have heard about Him. Maybe the miracle of the blind beggar proceeded their arrival. The bottom line is that wherever Jesus went, a crowd was sure to follow, and this was no exception. I can imagine the couple leaving the coffee table. The daily customer stopped talking mid-sentence, and the storeowner closing up shop, exclaiming Jesus is here! The crowd came and gathered to Jesus possibly along with the sick and the needy as demonstrated in previous examples when the Son of God entered a city. Everyone ostensibly wanted to *see* Jesus, and Zacchaeus wasn't any exception. The chief tax collector came across a sensitive issue, that being because he was a short man. He literally couldn't see above the crowd. Verse 3 says, "He wanted to *see* who Jesus was, but being a short man he could not, because of the crowd." He had obstacles to overcome if he wanted to see and catch a glimpse of Jesus. He came up short literally and had to get above the crowd. He wasn't seeking after Jesus, but he simply wanted to see him.

He simply desired to see, perceive, or observe but not to encounter. He just wanted to see him, not meet him. Maybe he was thinking who would want to meet him anyway? The tax collector spent that time in his life among people who didn't want anything to do with him. He didn't receive happy birthday cards, and some wished he wasn't born. He wasn't greeted with smiles and celebratory words but with whispers and disappointing scowls. Some may not have even knew his name, but they just knew his issues. His lifestyle gained many possessions but not a lot of love. Why would he think that Jesus would view him any differently? Why would anyone want to have a relationship with a crooked bill collector, misusing his power for personal gain? I believe that Zacchaeus was longing for community. He was anxious to find love and acceptance yet wasn't willing to uproot himself from the lifestyle he was living. Being a tax collector wasn't, the issue; it was the criminal actions he committed using that title as a tool. He had all the money but money in itself can't counsel you when you're lost, comfort you when you're lonely, or encourage you when you're down. The infamous Zacchaeus was like a celebrity who had everything but nothing. Maybe he owned everything thing money can buy but possessed nothing that money couldn't purchase. He had a cycle of hurt and perceived need that he couldn't change or he would lose everything. If I quit my cheater behavior or change my lifestyle, how will I stay wealthy; all that I have or know will be lost. Sin will lie to you and say that you have everything, but you have nothing.

With the taller bodies impeding his vision, he knew that he had to remedy the obstruction. Zacchaeus was desperate to see Jesus because he decided to climb a sycamore-fig tree to see him. Desperate times called for desperate measures.

FIND HIGHER GROUND

When watching survival shows or receiving survival training, the instructors will tell you that if you are lost in the wilderness, then you need to find higher ground. Seek out higher ground, so you can get your vision free of obstacles and see where you need to go or where you need to be heading. For some, it could be climbing up a mountain or a high hill. In jungles and tree-abundant environments or landscapes, it could be climbing up a tree. One of my favorite shows is called "*Man vs Wild*" by Bear Grylls. He talks about and demonstrates this often in his episodes. You have to take a break from just cutting though trees yet not having any vision as to where you are heading. He would often climb up a tree or high place to *see* his destination, so he can come down and *seek* out a path to reach it. Gaining higher ground helps us to see how to navigate in the wilderness. The vital fact that must be told is that in order to survive, you can't stay on the mountaintop or on top of the tree. Those encounters are meant to give perspective and vision. The growth and life in most landscapes happen in the valley. In order to reach the goal, task, or promise, you can't jump from one tree to another to avoid the valley. The valley is hard, sweaty, and trying work, but growth happens there. The battle happens in the valley, not on the mountaintop. The victory occurs in the valley not on the top of trees. When David came to deliver the food that his father Jesse gave him and check on the battle, they were only lined up for battle on top of a hill. However nothing was being won; nothing was being conquered. Twice a day for forty days the Israelites would do nothing but yell at the Philistines. The victory didn't happen on the top of the hill. The battle was waged, fought, and won as a young boy stepped into the valley with a covenant with God, equipped with a sling and stones. He killed the giant in the place of hardship, not the state of comfortability. David himself wrote about his understanding of the valley in the renowned passage of scripture in Psalm 23:4, saying, *"Even though I walk through the darkest valley I will fear no evil, for you are with me; your rod and your staff, they comfort me."*

In some places, trees or obstructions impeding vision wasn't the issue but simply not knowing where to go. Therefore, the requirement is to find a fixed, unmoving landmark and move toward that direction. In deserts where water is vital, a landmark is chosen that shows signs that water is in that direction. This is powerful, knowing that when we are lost and we don't know where to go, we have an unmoving and unchanging God who beckons us to walk, run, and if we are honest, sometimes trip and fall toward him. Hebrews 12:2 says, *"2fixing our eyes on Jesus, the **pioneer** and perfecter of faith. For the joy set before him he endured the cross, scorning its shame, and sat down at the right hand of the throne of God."*

Jesus is the fixed, unmoving, and always consistent rock in our life. He wants us to fix our eyes upon His life as we navigate the wilderness of life. Jesus is our pioneer. *Pioneer* means someone who has explored, or went before uncharted territories. Jesus knows the path well because He already walked it. Not only can He get us to it, but He can get us through it.

The tax collector may have thought he was climbing the tree just to see, but that act of unbeknown faith was an act of survival. As people were crowding Jesus to see, meet, and talk to Him, there in the distance was a man short in stature, climbing up a tree perhaps thinking surely Jesus is too busy with the people around him to notice me. What Zacchaeus didn't know was something that stops Him in His track and gains His attention is desperation and acts of faith. The woman with the issue of blood broke through a crowd to touch the edge of his cloak. In that moment, desperation and hunger was evident. In this powerful passage of scripture in Mark 5:24–34, Jesus tells her, "Daughter, your faith has healed you." Desperation and faith gains the attention of God. To the blind man's encounter on the way to Jericho when he shouted out, not to simply gain Jesus's attention, but to gain His audience, face-to-face with Jesus, He told him "Your faith has healed you." Maybe the tax collector didn't realize that he was setting himself up for an encounter that would change his life. Maybe he was just curious or maybe he was desperate; however, it doesn't change the fact that Jesus answers radical faith. He was seeing Jesus like a hunter in a tree stand as Jesus was walking toward him. Finally, Jesus reached the spot that Zacchaeus was at looked him and shared words that will not only change the tax collector's life, but shake the crowd around him. *"Zacchaeus, come down immediately, I must stay at your house today."* Heart beating rapidly, the palm of his hands perspired sweat, he thought, *Was Jesus talking to me?* "Zacchaeus come down immediately" was replaying over and over in his mind as time seemed to stand still. *Jesus is talking to me* he thought. Put yourself in the middle of the canvas of this situation. A crowd of people wanted to meet and have an encounter with the famous Jesus, only to see him call out the infamous tax collector. Imagine the whispers and the gasps of air as if his word removed the oxygen from the city. Jesus not only wanted the thief to come down but also to stay at his house. *Zacchaeus only wanted to see Jesus but Jesus was there to* seek *after him.* After the short man pinched himself to make sure this wasn't a dream, he came down the tree at once, and the Bible states that Zacchaeus welcomed Jesus gladly. There was a longing for community, a hunger for acceptance, and a deeply rooted impulse for love. Now the man is looking at love face to face. He had spent most of his adult life polishing his trophies, but now he is looking at the head that would bare a crown. The audience was floored that Jesus would make such a request. They didn't approve of the tax collector's lifestyle and so thought it was best to shun him. Jesus didn't approve of the tax collector's sinful lifestyle but welcomed him. Why? Because Jesus back then and still today loves the sinner and hates the sin. How did Jesus know Zacchaeus's name? Was it a word of knowledge or was his name infamously just known? Climbing down from the tree like stepping out from the pew or seat in a church service, he made his way to his altar call at the invitation from Jesus. The short man went from being an observer to having an encounter. The encounter didn't happen on the tree but in his valley among the ungodly fruit of his labor, a community of people who hated him—yet God was calling him. In this compelling moment before Jesus could say another word, he started to repent. His perspective and heart changed during the journey from the tree with the landmark of love and grace. As if years and days became seconds, he recalled his actions in his past and drew the conclusion that it is not worth staying the same. The encounter was changing him. He repented to Jesus around everyone as witnesses to his emotional display of Jesus's overwhelming love. He didn't simply say, "I am sorry"; he truly repented. *True repentance isn't simply apologizing it is the changing of lifestyle.* Verse 3 says, *"Here and now I give half of my possessions to the poor, and if I have cheated anybody out of anything, I will pay back four times the amount."* He weighed the options and hypothesized that Jesus was worth the effort to change. *"Jesus said to him, "Today salvation has come to this house, because this man, too, is a son of Abraham. [10] For the Son of Man came to seek and to save the lost."* So many people in the crowd who sinned differently than the tax collector didn't think that he deserved the encounter with Jesus. This speaks to the heart of a loving Savior who still chases after the unwanted and the unloved. Jesus, very attentive to his words, tells not only Zacchaeus but addresses the crowd stating "The man is also a son of Abraham." Putting myself in this story, like the backdrop of a movie, I am imagine tears running down the Zacchaeus's face. Regardless of the actions of his past, he still has the same blood as everyone else. He has the same covenant promise as everyone in the crowd. Jesus told him and everyone else that *he belongs*. Keeping in mind that Zacchaeus ushered many of these problems via the invitation of his actions. Yet in spite of it all, love covered him, and love reminded him that he belongs. Zacchaeus was set up from the start. The tax collector was only trying to *see* yet Jesus was there to *seek* after him. Not only did he seek after him, but his life was changed forever. *To see means to observe only, but to seek is to look for with a purpose.* Don't water down your faith to only seeing Jesus from a distance, creating the man-made obstacle, but *seek* after him and remove the excuses. This was Zacchaeus's reality as communicated, *"For the Son of Man came to* seek *and to* save *what was lost."* Jesus is still chasing after us. He didn't climb up a tree; He was hung upon a tree to save us, forgive us, redeem us, and empower us. He bore His crown on the cross of Calvary and set the example for love and sacrifice for all of us, showing the fact that crowns are greater than trophies

From Rags to Riches

Again, money and wealth wasn't the factor or sin in Zacchaeus; it was how he acquired it. Money isn't the root of all evil; it is the love of money that is the root of all evil as the scripture states. For years of his life, he put more value in money than his integrity. He put more worth in a bill or coin than what was ethical and more value in a tarnishing trophy filled with things rather than community. However, in the place of encounter with Jesus, he came to his senses that he needed to change his lifestyle. How did he change? It was via an encounter with a loving and grace-filled, God who wanted a relationship with him. Jesus won him over with an act of love not an act of aggression. He finally realized that he would rather have people in his life than a large house with no one in it. His encounter with the one who would bare a crown caused him to question his trophies in life. All that he had gained came with a price tag that he paid for years. What he thought was worthless was actually priceless. He eyes were opened, and Jesus didn't have to say a word. The tax collector went from rags to riches, rags being the things he had and riches being the love he gained. For so long, the pursuit of things caused him to miss out on so much more in life, which was something money can't buy even though he had a large bank account and he could afford to cover the check.

It is extremely important that we don't become so focused on gaining that we don't give attention on the things that we are losing. There is nothing wrong with wealth, money, success, or riches. The trepidation that should be seared in the hearts of every person is that we don't lose sight of the crown along with the way. Simply put, we can't buy everything with money. When you die, you can make plans for a golden casket but who will be at your funeral? Your kids may appreciate the new basketball shoes, but at what cost; is it costing them the price of you not being at their games, rooting them on, and cheering in the crowd? The house may be spotless and look like an episode off the HGTV channel, but do people want to visit due to the stressful atmosphere you set regarding keeping the house spotless? Gaining the American dream yet having no one to live the dream out with is a lonely road. We must fight to provide for our families but we also shouldn't lose them in the process.

SEEK AND TO SAVE

Maybe you found yourself at this very crossroad—finding out the trophy isn't worth it anymore. Perhaps you gained so much in life but used family as the dice rolled gambling, will they still be there after you gain the world? In my years of youth ministry and traveling as an evangelist, there is a truth that is very apparent. Many kids don't believe that their parents love them. From conversations after service, to the suicide letter handed to us after they got saved, all share simple words. They don't love me or care about me. Parents are absent; present at home but vacant in their life. "If I would die, they wouldn't even miss me or know I was gone." This chapter is a plea with you as the reader to pause in the busyness of your family and spend time with them. Don't believe for a moment that the amazing house that you provided can take the place of a loving home. Don't assume that they are okay because you can write a check to the problem. Sometimes they don't need a dollar they need an ear. Don't just *see* them; *seek* after them. I pray that you experience a grace in your family to confront and overcome the hindrances that are blocking the progress in your home. Step one is to direct your attention back to your family. They will assure you that the crown you wear as a parent is sometimes more important to them than the trophies that are needed at home. In this state of life, it isn't providing or parenting; it is parenting while providing. It is as a tight rope that many walk every day. You may fall every now and then, but there is a safety rope that will catch you. Just make sure you climb back up the tree once again to walk your way back down to the life that is happening around you.

CHAPTER 6
COVER IT, HIDE IT, BLAME IT

Breaking generational curses doesn't transpire by happenstance but by attention. Oftentimes it is a conscious action, borne of a desire to not pick up and pass down unwanted behaviors. It is stepping into the gap and saying enough is enough. It is carrying out a mission in which your consistent actions are the taskforce, aligning with the undertaking of stopping the cycle. Breaking generational curses is fostering an inward tenacity to say, "I am sick and tired of being sick and tired." When a person makes up in their mind and heart to achieve and reach their goals, nothing seems like it can stop them. A made-up mind with a laser-focused heart, pointed toward change is a powerful tool. Like a steam engine in a train, the pressure within thrusts the fixated individual toward breakthrough. A fed-up person will draw a line in the sand and take a stand. I am so thankful that my father did this same thing.

My father Kenneth broke the pattern of alcoholism and tobacco addiction and stood on the other side of the battlefield victorious. I vividly remember traveling when I was little to see family, only to arrive smelling a strong stench of smoke and heading upstairs to visit a family member with a cigar in one hand, alcohol in the other while wearing an oxygen tube. Whatever actions happened in my father's childhood while around the substances fueled him to put it to an end? Nevertheless, what could he do? Even though he didn't have control of the people around him, he had control over himself. How did he break the cycle of behavior? Simple; he didn't partake in it and when he raised us, he didn't bring it into our home. I was never tempted with getting drunk or even drinking, as it wasn't a model of behavior in my home. Now I have the honor to carry down this crown of victory, as my son will not see those substances in our home. Whether predisposed to alcoholism or not, my family is better off without it. It all started when my dad stepped into the battlefield, armored up with drive and wielding a sword of conviction. He waged war on the desires of the flesh and won, standing over the carcass with one foot placed on the body of addictions and two raised fists in the act of victory. Kings Ahaziah, Joash, Amaziah, and Uzziah failed to step up to the plate and swing toward the genetic adversity lofted toward them. None of them confronted the pattern of behavior, so their children didn't end up like the generations before them. Breaking the generational issues would not be mended by a prayer request alone but my constant actions girded up in that prayer.

Jesus Paid the Price

Galatians 3:13–14

"Christ hath redeemed us from the curse of the law, being made a curse for us: for it is written, Cursed is every one that hangeth on a tree: That the blessing of Abraham might come on the Gentiles through Jesus Christ; that we might receive the promise of the Spirit through faith."

That act of love demonstrated on the Cross of Calvary by our Savior Jesus Christ was life-changing. He is our greatest example of an individual stepping into the gap for people He loves, that is, everyone—even though many didn't love him in return. Jesus's love wasn't predicated from the permission slip of someone's approval. He is the very definition of love and sacrifice. He is the calm in our storm, the anchor in the wind. He is the sunrise in the darkest nights and the shelter on the hottest trying days. He is the blanket warming our spirit when life gives a cold shoulder and the breeze through labor-intensive battles. He is an elevator lifting our soul in times of depression and the encouraging friend during seasons of victory. He is the general, directing us during times of war in our minds, and he is the counselor navigating during sensitive family issues. He is love in flesh and love in deed. He is *Jesus,* the chain breaker, yoke remover, that is on the side of truth. He is faithful at His word and arrives at the beckon of His name. He is *Jesus,* and He is fighting for us. He knew that He had to step in and break the curse. Born to die, our precious Savior wrapped himself in flesh and entered this world with an assignment, a mission, and drive to break the cycle of sin and redeem mankind from its bondage. Galatians 5:21 says, "God made him who had no sin to be sin for us, so that in him we might become the righteousness of God."

Mi Casa Es Su Casa

The issues that we are all dealing with and fighting today all started with two people in the garden of Eden. The first few chapters of Genesis contain the accounts of creation. Before there was the moon and the stars, there was God. There wasn't a tree thrusting forth out of the earth. The terrain was barren and without life until God saw it was fitting. All creation was spoken into existence. As sounds vibrated out of the vocal cords of our Deity to His figurative tongue, He articulated the world into existence by His words. "Let there be" became the prelude that led the way as darkness was painted over with light. God was and still is a master artist, still molding and sculpting perfection. Like a brush in the hands of painter, He colored life on a canvas of nothingness. Using His words as the paint that we now appreciate as color and the beauty of His splendor. He spoke water, land, the sun, and the moon into existence. He declared with those same three words "Let there be" as animals and plant life sprang up. "Let there be" the thundering commanded that caused cells to stand at attention and follow orders. He created matter even before matter mattered. The Big Bang was only His little whisper as life was created. God being the ultimate administrator hung the earth close enough from the sun to receive its warmth yet far enough that it would not go up in flames. He created the law of gravity that keeps his creation stable and seasons that keeps the earth fruitful. He, the Savior, created perfection when he created earth. It is amazing to think that He did all of that to simply create a backdrop for his greatest creation: mankind. Humans were the only creation that God didn't merely speak into existence but He touched. From the dust of the ground, He molded and shaped man like a potter at a potter's wheel. The master was literally creating His masterpiece. Us! Simply put a piece of the Master. He didn't mold man with clay of imperfection or flaws; he used his own image as the blueprint of His children. His hands containing his rhetorical fingerprints were branded in our very purpose and core. We were created in his likeness and sketched from his identity. God then with a deep breath or a gentle nudge blew the breath of life into dirt mounds of a body.

> From the dust of the ground, He molded and shaped man like a potter at a potter's wheel. The master was literally creating His masterpiece. Us! Simply put a piece of the Master.

The curtains opened to start this play called life, and there stood Adam the first man. He proceeded to place Adam in a place of paradise and harvest abundant home, called the garden of Eden. He placed Adam in the exquisite garden and told him to work it and to take care of it. He was commanded to subdue and guard the land. Adam was also given the responsibility to name all the animals. Residing in paradise fulfilling the task and assignments God had given him, he had no care in the world. He was allowed to eat anything in the garden but not of the fruit from the tree of knowledge of good and evil. Life was perfect and possibility didn't seem like it could get any better. Yet there came a time when God saw it fit that it wasn't good for man to be alone and by himself, so he put Adam to sleep to create his wife Eve. God took a rib of Adam and created his helpmate and life partner: a woman named Eve. Life was perfect, and there wasn't a care in the world. Adam and Eve had each other and a close relationship with God. So close that God himself would walk in the garden. God didn't create man to stare at him from a distance but to have a relationship with his children.

DID GOD REALLY SAY?

In the garden of Eden, lurking about was Satan, formed as a snake hanging around the tree of man's compromise, the tree of the knowledge of good and evil. God gave Adam and Eve one rule: Do not eat of that tree. It was here, in this garden, that one meal would be the downfall that would be connected to mankind. They followed the Lord's commands without question and never pondered or desired the tree until it was presented to them. Walking in the cool breeze and thick brushes of the garden, they came to the location the tree was rooted in. Knowing that they weren't supposed to eat of this tree or even touch it, yet they were near it. As they approached the tree, the serpent began calling out to Eve. Now mankind is engaged in conversation with the tempter who uses words as weapons. One question out of the enemy's mouth persuaded Eve to question everything that God had said:

> Genesis 3:1
>
> "Now the serpent was more crafty than any of the wild animals the Lord God had made. He said to the woman, "Did God really say, 'You must not eat from any tree in the garden'?"

"Did God really say?" One question that was presented to mankind at the start of creation that is still being rehearsed—the thought that is pondered right before the place of compromise. They stepped back from the deep conviction of knowing what is right to dabble in wrong behavior. Their moral compass was being swayed by the magnetized pull of temptation. The devil is a salesman who can sell water to the ocean. He will present you things you don't really need, but there will always be a price tag that will cost you more than you intended to pay. The Bible states that Eve saw that the fruit was good for food and pleasing to the eye. Her entire perspective shifted from one pondered question: did God really say? It was at this moment that Eve thought about the pros and cons of eating the fruit. Hell was screaming with excitement as the fall of man was near. As the fruit approached her mouth, ungodly applauses and cheers were given below, as those actions would become sin's welcome mat. She ate the fruit and gave some to her husband. The red carpet was laid out as sin arrived in this world.

Cover, Hide, and Blame

Genesis 3:6–12

> "When the woman saw that the fruit of the tree was good for food and pleasing to the eye, and also desirable for gaining wisdom, she took some and ate it. She also gave some to her husband, who was with her, and he ate it. [7] Then the eyes of both of them were opened, and they realized they were naked; so they sewed fig leaves together and made coverings for themselves. [8] Then the man and his wife heard the sound of the Lord God as he was walking in the garden in the cool of the day, and they hid from the Lord God among the trees of the garden. [9] But the Lord God called to the man, "Where are you?" [1]0 He answered, "I heard you in the garden, and I was afraid because I was naked; so I hid." [1]1 And he said, "Who told you that you were naked? Have you eaten from the tree that I commanded you not to eat from?" [1]2 The man said, "The woman you put here with me—she gave me some fruit from the tree, and I ate it."

Shame and guilt were new emotions that they had never felt before. The deep-pitted feeling of knowing something is wrong will now become a feeling that will keep them company. When they noticed that they were naked and uncovered, they attempted to put matters in their own hands. Adam and Eve being budget seamstresses sewed fig leaves together. Through their own efforts, they attempted to cover up their nakedness. As we all have done in a place of compromise, we try to fix it ourselves. Suddenly, they heard the moving of branches or the crackling of leaves in the distance. It was God walking in the garden. It wouldn't have been an issue before as it was an expected part of the day. However, Adam and Eve started a love triangle, dated sin, and they were about to be caught. Futile as it may be, they attempted to hide.

Reading this seems as if they were ridiculous for trying to hide from God, but we do this same thing all the time. When a person makes a mistake, sometimes they will attempt to do three things, cover it up, hide it, and blame others. We try to fix it ourselves and cover up the fact that we failed. We put on a mask in church, acting like everything is perfect, knowing that there is mess going on. We're spending time on Sunday morning putting on "Christian-ish makeup," Applying the "I'm too blessed to be stressed foundation" and smearing the "Glory be to God and I know how to shout" mascara. We are wearing the lipstick of "falling out under the power and come on, somebody," painting a picture of having church, going to church, all the while never addressing the pain within. We are walking into a building just to perform but not to be transformed. We will foolishly try to cover up our pain for the benefit of the opinions of the people around us, yet refuse to present ourselves in a fashion that gains the attention of the God above us. He sees us and knows our current circumstance, yet still desires us to come to Him.

Imagine going to the doctor's office because you are having stomach problems. The physician asks you what is wrong or what are your symptoms, and you tell him you have a headache. The fact that we have falsified our symptoms hinders the doctor from meeting out the need we have. So we will leave the doctor's office in pain and disappointed. We then will have the nerve to believe that the doctor didn't help, even though deep within we know we weren't honest. Every Sunday, there are people spiritually dying in the waiting room and lobby of a hospital, never getting to lie on the Great Physician's operating table. Why? It is not because Jesus isn't willing, but because we aren't being real and not because the pastor isn't preaching the Word, but because we are rejecting the medicine acting like we don't need it. Adam and Eve covered up their shame through their own efforts, yet God could see right through the mask. Adam and Eve struggled to hide from God to no avail. There truly isn't anything new under the sun. Identical behaviors are still being exercised in our era. The weight of guilt and shame connected to ungodly actions drives some into hiding. Typically, though they are very active in their local church and ministry, they drift away. Like a crab tucked into its shell, they go into hiding from the eyes of unknowing people. They rehearse the constant thought that others can see what is going on in their life, and they aren't perfect. Sadly, they are hiding, so they won't be seen, and others will not ask the question "Where have you been?" Instead of confronting the pain within and the twisted view and guilt, they would rather run away. Adam and Eve attempted a foolish game of hide-and-seek, not knowing that God would always seek them even if they were to go into hiding. There isn't a place or a state in life when Jesus is not chasing after us. Hide-and-seek driven by guilt and shame is an imprudent and irrational endeavor as He will be standing at your destination with an outstretched arm and open hand to receive you back to Himself.

> Adam and Eve attempted a foolish game of hide-and-seek, not knowing that God would always seek them even if they were to go into hiding.

Psalm 138:1–18

1 "You have searched me, Lord,
 and you know me.
2 You know when I sit and when I rise;
 you perceive my thoughts from afar.
3 You discern my going out and my lying down;
 you are familiar with all my ways.
4 Before a word is on my tongue
 you, Lord, know it completely.
5 You hem me in behind and before,
 and you lay your hand upon me.

⁶ Such knowledge is too wonderful for me,
  too lofty for me to attain.
⁷ Where can I go from your Spirit?
  Where can I flee from your presence?
⁸ If I go up to the heavens, you are there;
  if I make my bed in the depths, you are there.
⁹ If I rise on the wings of the dawn,
  if I settle on the far side of the sea,
¹⁰ even there your hand will guide me,
  your right hand will hold me fast.
¹¹ If I say, "Surely the darkness will hide me
  and the light become night around me,"
¹² even the darkness will not be dark to you;
  the night will shine like the day,
  for darkness is as light to you.
¹³ For you created my inmost being;
  you knit me together in my mother's womb.
¹⁴ I praise you because I am fearfully and wonder-
  fully made;
  your works are wonderful,
  I know that full well.
¹⁵ My frame was not hidden from you
  when I was made in the secret place,
  when I was woven together in the depths of
  the earth.
¹⁶ Your eyes saw my unformed body;
  all the days ordained for me were written
  in your book
  before one of them came to be.
¹⁷ How precious to me are your thoughts, God!
  How vast is the sum of them!
¹⁸ Were I to count them,
  they would outnumber the grains of sand—
  when I awake, I am still with you."

Adam and Eve couldn't hide from God, and we can't either. Nowhere on the earth is a place that His gaze can't reach. There is no depth of darkness where His light can't penetrate. No fortress built with bricks of shame is so strong that His grace can't tear it down. Yet even though we know all of these truths, we still attempt to hide anyway. Adam and Eve modeled this foolish attempt of hiding from a God who knows everything. He created longitude and latitude; surely He is aware of the location of the two most significant creatures He created. God, drawing near to Adam and Eve, asked a set up question, requiring them to share their current state of awareness. God asked, "Where are you?" Finally, they spoke up and said they were naked and afraid, so they hid. Fear was another emotion that was new to them and ushered by one sinful act of disobedience. Fear, shame, and guilt are triplets that always move together. If one is present, you can bet that the others are there. God asked the direct question of who told them they were naked. He also reminded them of his simple command not to eat the fruit.

The first man and woman began to disclose all that happened to them in the recent moments. However, the first thing out of Adam's mouth in his current sinful state was to point fingers and to blame others:

Genesis 3:12

The man said, "The woman you put here with me—
she gave me some fruit from the tree, and I ate it."

Adam blamed Eve and even made a remark to God, reminding Him that He put her here. The floods of emotion and feelings happening to Adam and Eve were hard to handle. There in the place of paradise, sin entered the world. Adam and Eve attempted to cover up their shame, hide from the one holding them accountable, and blame others for their actions. Truly, these are all behaviors acted out in everyday life. God addressed the serpent in the garden and cursed him. He shared with Adam and Eve the consequences that sin welcomed. To Eve, bearing a child would be painful, and there will be a desire to rule over her husband. To Adam, the task of working the ground for food would be difficult. Both Adam and Eve would experience the intense pain of labor—labor in childbirth and labor in providing for his family. Life literally just got a lot harder for mankind.

Redeeming Mankind

Yet in spite of all of the recent actions, God had redemption in mind. As a father that sees his children's mistakes, He still desires a relationship. From the start of sin, God was conversing with Jesus to conquer it. No boundary and no hindrance were going to keep our heavenly Father from His children. This deep crevice had to be bridged, and the anchoring points from one end of the chasm to the other would be a rugged bloody cross. God had redemption in mind, not only to cover up their shame, but to restore them. His actions would bring mankind out of hiding and into the open fields of His grace and love. The impulse to blame others would not be necessary as Jesus would carry the weight of shame for us. Jesus would conquer the curse of sin. The price of this great transition would literally be paid in blood—not the blood of mankind but the blood of the One who created mankind.

Genesis 3:21

"The Lord God made garments of skin for Adam and his wife and clothed them".

Why would God take the time to cover up Adam and Eve even though they were already covered? Adam and Eve sewed fig leaves together to cover up their nakedness. Yet the Lord killed an animal and made garments of skin to cloth His children.

Hebrews 9:22

"In fact, the law requires that nearly everything be cleansed with blood, and without the shedding of blood there is no forgiveness".

Bloodshed was already happening to redeem mankind. Later in history, priests would make animal sacrifices in the temple for the forgiveness of sins. Yet, even after that, a final sacrifice would take place that would end the need for any other bloodshed. Jesus Christ would walk the earth performing miracles and being the outstretched arms of God. Three and a half years into his ministry, He would hang on the cross to die for the sins for all mankind. Sin would be conquered, and Jesus would break generational curses. He was the last Adam who fixed the first Adam's mistake. Adam and Eve were kicked out of the garden of Eden and away from the tree of life. However, little did they know that one day the Giver of life would hang on a tree to preserve life.

CHAPTER 7
CONFRONT IT, FACE IT, OVERCOME IT

There is a lie that plagues our day-to-day lives. It is the notion that some pains, wounds, and issues go away with time. However, they do not go away with time but harvest deep-rooted implosive, and at times, explosive actions. Coincidentally, the only aspect that goes away is the opportunity to confront, face, and overcome it. This is a prodigious notion that God understood. If He was going to redeem mankind from the wages of sin, then actions must be taken, not mental accent or wishful thinking. Nor was it a procrastinating attitude toward the recent sinful cancer that now found a host in Adam and Eve. The remedy wasn't going to found in programs, debates, or mind-over-matter exercises. The problem wasn't an issue that man could write a check for or talk their way out off. Jesus knew at that moment and even before that that he would be born with the purpose to die.

Philippians 2:8

[8] And being found in appearance as a man, He humbled Himself and became obedient to the point of death, even the death of the cross

Motived by passion to reconcile the relationship between God and man, Jesus stepped into the earth with a mission. He didn't come for a church service, but He came to serve us. Something was wrong with his creation. He, being the manufacturer, molded us out of the dirt and breathed life into us. Thus, the Master who created His master-piece would be willing to get his hands dirty once again. He had dirt under his nails and on His hands when he molded us in the soil at the time of creation. He would later have the dirt and filth on His open, wounded hands. Blood would cover the three nails used to anchor him on the cross. Jesus would have his first birthday, aware of his funeral. Yet in the life and ministry of Jesus He never preached at a funeral, not even his own. Why? Because He brings dead things back to life. At the start of creation, throughout history and still today, Jesus has always been willing to get his hands dirty to free his children from the wages of sin. He will and He has stepped into the gap fighting for mankind.

Wrote on the Dirt

John 8

[1] but Jesus went to the Mount of Olives.
[2] At dawn he appeared again in the temple courts, where all the people gathered around him, and he sat down to teach them. [3] The teachers of the law and the Pharisees brought in a woman caught in adultery. They made her stand before the group [4] and said to Jesus, "Teacher, this woman was caught in the act of adultery. [5] In the Law Moses commanded us to stone such women. Now what do you say?" [6] They were using this question as a trap, in order to have a basis for accusing him. But Jesus bent down and started to write on the ground with his finger. [7] When they kept on questioning him, he straightened up and said to them, "Let any one of you who is without sin be the first to throw a stone at her." [8] Again he stooped down and wrote on the ground.
[9] At this, those who heard began to go away one at a time, the older ones first, until only Jesus was left, with the woman still standing there. [10] Jesus straightened

up and asked her, "Woman, where are they? Has no one condemned you?"
¹¹ "No one, sir," she said.
"Then neither do I condemn you," Jesus declared. "Go now and leave your life of sin."

Jesus, doing what He was gifted and anointed to do, was teaching when all of sudden drama "popped off." Religious people known as Pharisees brought into the gathering a woman caught in the very "*act*" of adultery. The *act*! While the slow jam music was being played, they dragged her out of her moment of sin to apparently face trial in front of Jesus. With the ill attempt to grab a woman who had sinned differently than they did, they sought to entrap Jesus to have a basis of accusing him. Little did they know Jesus was who He said He was; He is the Son of God. While they may have only known of this woman at her moment of weakness, Jesus knew of her before she was even formed, being present when they (the Godhead) knit her together in her mother's womb, sowing in her purpose using threads of hope, love, and grace. He was there in her high times, and He was present in her low times. They foolishly attempted to trap Jesus, but all they did was create a spotlight so Jesus would display His love to all those around. While others had destruction in mind, Jesus had redemption. They viewed her as trash, but Jesus knew of His recycling program. When a person puts an item in the trash, we recognize that it is empty, broken, used up, and simply doesn't have a function. Simply put, its current state yields no present purpose. Conversely, when we put that same item in the recycle bin, we acknowledge similar truths. Yes, it is used up, broken, and empty, but we place it in the recycle bin because there's an understanding that regardless of its present state or its past, it still has future worth. All that is needed is a process for it to be recreated and "*born again*."

Now, present and desperate stood a woman, whom by law should be stoned to death. The Pharisees questioned Jesus, yet He didn't say a word. Suddenly Jesus, the Son of God, bent down and started to write in the dirt, getting His hands dirty for a woman covered in the dirt of her own shame. The Bible doesn't communicate what was written in the dirt. Yet whatever it was, it was powerful. They continued to question Jesus, and He made a powerful and thought-provoking statement: "If anyone of you is without sin, let him be the first to throw a stone at her." I can imagine the facial expressions of bloodthirsty individuals shifted when hearing those words. Jesus went back to writing on the dirt with the dirt under His nails in front of the woman who was counting down the last moments of her life. Anticipating the stones that would be hurled toward her knowing that there wasn't a way out of this, she had gotten herself into a place where only Jesus could free her. In what could only seem like a lifetime to the desperate woman, one by one, the Pharisees dropped their stones. Every thud the stones made on the dusty ground would have given this woman a feeling of relief, knowing that that particular stone wouldn't be the projectile that ended her life. Finally, after the dust had settled and all the religious Pharisees had left, Jesus straightened up, took his hands out of the dirt, and put his attention on her. The only man who had the résumé qualified to stone her was Jesus himself. However, He didn't come to kill her; he came to rescue her. He got dirty and stood up for her; better yet, He humbled himself to touch what she was crawling in. Just as the woman with the issue of blood, we all, as unclean people, can touch a clean God, and He restores us. With the same mission in mind, He liberated her from death via stoning and commanded her to leave her life of sin. Jesus wasn't out to destroy the woman; He was out to destroy sin. The resolution is still present: to redeem mankind from the wages of sin. Jesus didn't ignore her sins; he freed her from its wages. God didn't ignore the separation that was created in the Garden of Eden: a lie that was whispered from the mouth of the deceiver on a tree, would be conquered by "The Truth" that would hang for three days on a tree. From this moment in scripture, with the woman caught in the act of adultery, from the garden of Eden, Jesus was fueled with a tenacity to resolve the first Adam's mistakes by being the last Adam. This burning drive is what led him to the cross in the first place. A separation was created, and only Jesus could mend it.

The Courtroom

Romans 5:18–19

Consequently, just as one trespass resulted in condemnation for all people, so also one righteous act resulted in justification and life for all people. [19] For just as through the disobedience of the one man the many were made sinners, so also through the obedience of the one man the many will be made righteous."

Just as any loving parent, they desire a relationship with their children. Great conflict happened at the start of creation and robbed God of that gift. Yet, He wasn't going to sit and not do anything, but rather He moved heaven and earth to bridge the gap. God, in creating man, desired to have a relationship with him. His kids broke the Father's heart; now He does whatever he can to bridge the gap, He came to break the curse that keeps Him away from His children. He doesn't want co-custody; He wants a fulltime relationship. Adam's mistake had consequences that transcended generations after him. They unwillingly welcomed the curse and bondage sin carried with it. One choice would change history. Just as Adam's choice echoed through time, Jesus would do the same. Yet it wasn't a choice to welcome the wages of sin, but a mission to abolish it. When He died on the cross and rose the third day, actions met sin and overpowered it. A wedge that was used to continually separate man from God would be uprooted by a Savior on the cross of Calvary. He would see His children through prison glass as the mistakes incarcerated man, but He would come as a lawyer pleading man's case, interceding for man's freedom from the chains of condemnation. The accuser of the brethren, also known as the father of lies, would point out the guilt of man and slam the evidence on the table. The fact would be true, and the mistakes would be unquestionable. Lying, gossip, slander, and lust—the list goes on and on. The accuser, being confident that the one on trial would be found guilty as the evidence is heavily weighed against him, brings up choices and regrets of the past, echoing the shame that was carried over time after time from those actions. Yet, even though the devil may see the facts of man's past, he would quickly notice that it was covered in blood. A covenant had been made with Jesus for the defendant's life. Dumbfounded with what has happened, the accuser would yell "I want the truth and nothing but the truth," and the *Truth* Himself, Jesus Christ, would stand up for man and speak on our behalf. Our lord and savior makes intercession for us. He fights in the courtroom. While the enemy points the finger, Jesus points at the holes in his hands and feet. As the accuser of the brethren focuses on the mistake, Jesus gives attention to the sacrifice. Jesus has fought for us, and He is still fighting for us. God didn't hide from or overlook the grave mistake of man, but He opposed it.

Generational Curses

There are issues in our lives that have been passed down from generation to generation, not passed down as in the sense of given as a family heirloom, but inherited by not giving attention to the issue. We all see it every day of our lives. He sees the fruit of it as we fight through the drama connected to it. If you would take a moment to think back on the history of your family, you can notice the same struggles from generation to generation. Maybe your great-grandfather was introduced to alcohol and would later become an alcoholic. This pattern of behavior was introduced and welcomed by your grandfather, and he walked in the shoes of that lifestyle, knowing very well the times his father would come home drunk and angry and the times that he would curse and yell while being intoxicated. Your grandfather was able to recall the bill driven up by the bondage to a bottle. Yet at the end of the day, he believed the lie that the bottle was the only thing that helped him relax. Thus, the grandfather would still carry over the same example to his son, as it was just how families acted. This cycle will be continued like a hamster on a wheel until someone says enough is enough—enough of the unruly action, enough of the unrestrained drinking, and enough of the drunk driving and forgotten actions and one-night stands. The son would make up in his mind that he would draw a line in the sand and refuse to touch a bottle and get drunk. Why? Because he noticed a pattern and gave attention to the results. This substance wasn't adding to his family's life, but it was taking peace, joy, and hope away from them. That is how we break generational curses. We overcome it and break it by our consistent actions and behaviors. By no means am I taking away from the power of an experience at the altar. One moment in the presence of God can change everything. Nevertheless, the question is, what you are going to do when the church service is over? What are you going to do when the pastor leaves and the "b3" organ is being played? What are you going to do when the choir has stepped off the risers? Too many people are frustrated at church, and when they leave church, it's because they are shouting for things and peace that they aren't willing to fight for. The times on the mountaintop of His presence are to prepare you to wage war on the issues of life in your valley. However, it starts and ends with a choice. Breaking generational curses starts with a choice. It is important to remember that Jesus Christ already died on the cross to redeem us from generational bondage and the wages of sin. So the question to ask is that if He did all those great exploits for me, then why are we still dealing with the same issues? We renew the pain by carrying over the actions. Jesus paved a way for us to be free, but He can't place us on that path; we have to walk on it. We have the free will to choose, a choice that He won't force us to make as in doing it for us, but He presents the corridor of liberty that He created when he conquered sin, death, and the grave. There is a real devil, demons, and a kingdom of darkness. However, sometimes we often give him credit for things that we do ourselves. We will say, "I am taking back everything the devil stole from me." But sadly, it wasn't an invasion; it was an infestation through an invitation. As long as our actions keep holding the door open to sin, we welcome it and all its depressing guests. Yes, there is power in prayer and fasting. Yes, there is a vital importance to soak your journey to freedom in prayer; however, no prayer in the world will affect your free will. You have to make up in your mind not to partake in the actions that have been consistently bringing you pain in the first place. It is time to break the cycle of behavior in your family. Why? Because crowns are greater than trophies. Don't be like the kings mentioned in previous chapters, but confront the elephant in the room. Give attention to the behavior that has ushered in so much pain in the past. Let your actions benefit that which is the world to you, just as the actions of the last Adam, Jesus, would benefit all the world. The actions you carry out today will affect your children and your future. Fight for your son by overcoming drugs. Fight for your daughter, not simply by fighting divorce, but by creating a healthy marriage. Fight for your future spouse by saving yourself for marriage. Fight for your children by antagonizing and combating the lust and porn addictions. Fight so the generations after you will benefit from your victories.

While I was writing this chapter in this book, a man walked into my office for counseling. He was telling me how the lust and ungodly behavior he was dealing with was affecting his marriage. He continued to tell me how his father dealt with the same thing and possibly the father before him. That's three generations of man struggling with the same things in detail. Who is going to break the cycle of behavior? I'll tell you; it's the one who is man enough to confront the issues trying to overtake and overwhelm him. He left my office with a mission in mind to fight this battle and win, not only for himself, but also for his children so that he is modeling a lifestyle of victory they can model after. What an amazing reminder that even as the words were fleshly typed on this document, a reminder of its truths steps into my office. You *can* break the cycle.

When sin entered the world, the first things Adam and Eve did were to "cover it, hide it, and blame it." They covered up their shame with fig leaves. They hid from God in fear and guilt when they heard God walking in the garden. Adam blamed his wife, and his wife blamed the serpent, yet neither ever looked at the person in the mirror. In order to break the pattern and cycle of behavior, we can't cover it, hide from it, or blame others for it. Now as we must give attention to the very sinful nature within us, we must *confront it, face it, and overcome* it.

Confront It

Proverbs 28:13

[13] Whoever conceals their sins does not prosper, but the one who confesses and renounces them finds mercy.

Just as with anything in life, the first step of repairing a problem is facing the fact that it exists. Acting like nothing is wrong or that it isn't a big deal will only aid in the continuation of the delinquent exploits. The problem must be dragged, kicking and screaming if need be, into the light, not swept under the rug with the hopes that it will disappear. It can't be joked off or masqueraded as if you're prancing though the clouds when truly you're pugnaciously creeping in the mud and mire of issues. Bring it into the light.

I grew up in a little town in North Carolina called Eden. This town was so small that when we finally got a Dollar Tree, people waited in line at the doors as if it was Black Friday to be the first ones to shop at it. I recall one day in my little country town, I went to the backyard to play outside. We had a pretty big backyard with plenty of room of a ten-year-old boy to run and play. I soon noticed that a plank of plywood was laying on the ground undisturbed for quite some time. I drew the conclusion from observing the grass under it had been robbed of light and became white and discolored. Curiosity got the best of me, so I decided to disturb the discarded wood by lifting it up from the ground. As soon as I raised it from the ground, I noticed an entire community of beetles, "roly polies," and earthworms scurrying about. I disturbed their rest. The point I am making is that they didn't start moving because I intimated them and talked junk about their momma; they didn't move because I threatened to step on them. They moved around because when I gave attention to the covering they were hiding and concealed under, the light invaded the darkness. Bring the issues into the light. Raise up the plank of wood covering your eyes and attention, and drag the sin and problem into the light. Because only then can the healing process start. It starts by finally saying this needs to change. It happens when you're being Jennifer Lopez in the movie *Enough* and train to fight what is beating on you. As the statement is exclaimed with the last nerve given and the cup of conflict is running over: "Enough is enough." We can no longer afford to act as if just because the pain has always been in the past, that it has to be endorsed in your present and expected in our future. Stop covering up the issues that need to be confronted. Stop being so concerned about the outward appearance of keeping up with the neighbors because they have issues, too. As the seasoned saints will say, "You can put makeup on a pig, but it is still a pig." The first step to usher the change needed in your life is to know that things need to change. However, if the fruit of pain is going to be killed outwardly, the seed needs to be uprooted internally. Even when the root of the pain can't be seen, it doesn't mean that it doesn't need attention.

In the Old Testament when the priest would minister in the temple, God gave strict instructions to their garments. In the book of Exodus, He instructs them to wear the ephod, the breastplate, and other priestly garments. After they got all dressed in God's attire, there was no question who they were and what they were called, instructed, and prepared to do. Yet with all the attention to the outer garments, God still saw it fit to instruct them about their undergarments, which was underwear and clothing that no one else would see and no one would know that they weren't wearing. Yet if it is important to God, then it should be important to us.

Exodus 28:42–43

[42] "Make linen undergarments as a covering for the body, reaching from the waist to the thigh. [43] Aaron and his sons must wear them whenever they enter the tent of meeting or approach the altar to minister in the Holy Place, so that they will not incur guilt and die.

God's attention to the garments of the priest wasn't solely on what others can see but also the items that no one else can. His concern was not only the things displayed in public but also the garments covered up in private. God believed in this so much that he communicated the punishment that would happen if they tried to minister without wearing their underwear. Attention needs to be given to what is acknowledged in public and have the integrity to be obedient to the things unseen. The pain acquired from forcing out the outward garment but not the secret and unseen issues are guilt and death. When Adam and Eve ate the fruit and death and sin entered into their lives, for the first time, the first thing they did was try to cover it up. Cover up what? The guilt and shame they felt due to their nakedness. The first step of breaking free from the generational pain passed down from family to family and offspring to offspring is to uncover and confront the issue. Don't put on your best priestly garment and move on in life as normal. Those actions have been modeled after you before, yet the problem is still overwhelmingly present. Be the one in your family, who turns around to see the pattern of pain in your past and then looks inward to access the mental and spiritual fortitude to combat the desire to cover, rather than confront. The nutrition that keeps generational curses alive is a square meal of silence and apathy washed down by a cup of guilt. Whatever unspoken rule exists that keeps others from facing the giant of bondage, prancing through family after family, needs to be stopped. Break the cycle by confronting the issue. Victoria has let the secret out now; what are you going to do with it?

Face It

Step one is to confront the issues, and step two is to face it. It's not enough to acknowledge the circumstance; it needs to be confronted. Breaking generational curses isn't fragmented by wishful thinking but by a prayer-driven tenacious drive. After Adam and Eve ate the fruit, they attempted to conceal their nakedness by fashioning makeshift fig leaf garments. God was walking in the garden, and they heard him approaching. In previous times, the encounter would have been celebrated, yet now it was dreaded. They attempted to hide from God, an action counseled by an uneducated teacher named condemnation that graduated from the university of guilt and shame. They tried to play a foolish game of hide and seek from a God who knows our tomorrow while it was yesterday. We must face the issue, not hide from it. It is paramount that you face the battle and your fight in it. How do you fight to break the cycle of bondage? It is not by fighting others; it is fighting and facing the desire within you. Galatians 5:17 says, *17" For the flesh desires what is contrary to the Spirit, and the Spirit what is contrary to the flesh. They are in conflict with each other, so that you are not to do whatever you want."*

The three kings in 2 Chronicles all had the same fight within them—three men with the same battles and the same wars, three crowns but the same blood lust for trophies. Sadly, at the end of the day, all of them were slain from the same champion of entitlement and pride. Why did it continue? It's because some didn't face it at all, and others faced it yet failed to continue to fight it. The fight isn't won by a glance; it is conquered by consistent attention. The two dogs within are called the flesh and the spirit. Whoever wins is completely determined by us. Whichever one we feed is the one that is going to win. The essential truth to comprehend is that you can't "bind" the flesh; you have to crucify it. Going to the altar to have hands laid on you to cast out your flesh simply will never happen. We have the authority to cast out demons and bind spirits but not flesh. We can cast out the spiritual influences trying to be a leech to our flesh. However, our flesh through diurnal choices and the grace that Jesus pours out to us is destroyed by our daily choice to deny it its meal.

Galatians 2:20

[20] I have been crucified with Christ and I no longer live, but Christ lives in me. The life I now live in the body, I live by faith in the Son of God, who loved me and gave himself for me.

This very well could be the reason why Sunday after Sunday you find yourself dealing with the same things after responding to altar call after altar call. Could it be because you haven't been walking in the disciplines demanded to see what you been shouting for? Effort is required even after the altar call is over. Even unsaved and unchurched people will quote the scripture "Faith without works is dead." Any who knows me knows that I strongly believe in the power of God and the transformation that can happen when we choose to respond to God. By His grace and mercy, we have seen deaf ears opened, blind eyes seeing, people raised up out of wheelchairs and other creative miracles. We have seen families restored and a multitude of souls saved when they answered an altar call and chased after Jesus. His power is very real, yet so are our actions. We have to get involved in our own freedom. We have to get beyond praying for the very things that Jesus has already empowered us to do. Pray for the strength, and He will give it to you. Pray for the grace, and he will pour it out on you. God enables us to fight; He doesn't pamper us to remain weak. Face your flesh and fight it by nailing it to the cross of Calvary. Understand that His finished work empowers us to walk in authority and gifts to no longer be a punching bag of the enemy but to wage war. The grace of God poured out on us doesn't grant us apathy to remain stagnant but rather to be fueled with an eager, ambitious drive to crusade though battlefields of pain, taking captive the terrorist being a sleeper cell of our lives while releasing the POW of peace suppressed for far too long. You have to get behind your own freedoms. Our sinful nature is crucified and starved by a choice just as much as it is fed and celebrated by choices.

Luke 9:23

[23] Then he said to them all: "Whoever wants to be my disciple must deny themselves and take up their cross daily and follow me.

To be a follower of Jesus, better known as a Christian, the Lord set clear parameters for us. The command is to deny ourselves, take up our cross, and follow him daily. First and foremost, Jesus makes the statement with the word *disciple*, not fan or groupie. A disciple is someone who is willing to learn, lead, serve, and follow, a person who will receive instructions but also correction. In His following instruction, he directs them to deny themselves. This means we have to give attention to the notion "if you feel like it, do it" and reject it because a feeling was never the permission slip to do it. We can't live life wearing the name of a Christian, receiving the joys of salvation, yet negating the responsibly of servants under His lordship. An understanding is clearly communicated that we must deny ourselves. God will not deny ourselves for us; that would overcome the standard of free will. You have the right to choose. We have the choice to turn our backs on Jesus or come to Him just as we are. We can say no to his leadership, or we can live our life under his guidance. We have to mature as children of God, not just sitting at the table of break-through, waiting for God to cut up the food of victory all the while He placed the knife in our hands. "Gaga gogos" is very cute when a person is one year old, but it is not cute when they are thirty-five. He is a Father who will teach us how to ride the bike called freedom. He is the same Father who will at times remove the spiritual goosebumps, remove the training wheels of a situation, and teach you how to ride without him holding on to the bike. Just as a father pushing his child on the back from behind, repeating the comforting words to the eager yet nervous child "I got you, I got you," reiterating the words to the forward focused child, He gradually lets go of the seat and stands in amazement to see his child ride the bike without assistance. I pray as you are facing the issues of your life, combating the generational curses and behavior, that you will hear the Father say over you, "I've got you; I've got you." God empowers you, but He will not pedal for you. Could it be maybe we have been expecting God to fix situations that we aren't willing to give our attention to or put our hands on? No, you have to get involved in our own deliverance.

Hebrews 12:1–3

"Therefore, since we are surrounded by such a great cloud of witnesses, let us throw off everything that hinders and the sin that so easily entangles. And let us run with perseverance the race marked out for us, [2] fixing our eyes on Jesus, the pioneer and perfecter of faith. For the joy set before him he endured the cross, scorning its shame, and sat down at the right hand of the throne of God.[3] Consider him who endured such opposition from sinners, so that you will not grow weary and lose heart."

A few keys words in verse one demands proper attention. The writing of Hebrews expresses foundational truths and is a reminder of getting involved in our own deliverance. Firstly, he said to let "us" throw off everything. It doesn't read: let God throw it off, but let us throw it off. Once we choose to throw it off and remove it, we then should place it in the hands of the One who welcomes our burden, pain, and issues. Throw it off and lay it down at Jesus's feet who states, "My burden is easy and My yoke is light." We must actively and attentively choose to throw off the hindrances and entanglements. Once again, please don't misread what I am telling you. I am not telling you that God won't intervene when you call out to Him. I am not saying that God won't lift a finger when you cry out to Him because He is present in our times of victories and our times of trouble. He will be your coach that empowered you by the Holy Spirit to "beat your flesh into submission." He will equip you to fight the fight of faith, but He won't fight your fight of faith for you. The stinky thinking is the false thought that He will reach down from heaven and lift your finger. Maybe you're praying for God to heal you from issues of blood sugar. As you're praying, keep in mind He won't stop you from driving through your favorite donut shop. He won't close your own hand as you reach for the sixth donut. As amazing as that gourmet donut taste is, we have to have self-control, which is a fruit of the Spirit. What God will do is aid you in cultivating that fruit within you, so you can say no when it is time to say no. It is time to throw off the hindrance, throw off the excuse, throw off the bondage, and put on the grace to face what you and maybe the generations before you have been running from for too long. *1 Peter 5:7, "Cast all your anxiety on him because he cares for you."*

Secondly, the verse from Hebrews 1 states to throw off everything that hinders. This is an important fact to know because in the fight of freedom, many times the stumbling blocks are issues that are perceived as dangerous but misused to cause the most harm. A hindrance in itself isn't a sin. Owning a TV isn't a sin, but what you watch on it could be. Owning a car isn't a sin, but where you go may be. Having money isn't a sin yet, as stated in a previous chapter, what you spend that money on could be. These are the problems hardest to spot. Sin is easily recognized, yet a hindrance isn't. Nonetheless, the word of God tells us to "throw off everything that hinders and the sin that so easy entangles us. We must give attention to what we put our attention into because on the other side of the door could be sin waiting and crouching, staking out an opportunity to make itself at home. Keeping in mind the nature of sin truly is a sloppy guest, and its personality is to rob, kill, and destroy. As you evaluate the pattern of behavior in your life and the generation before you, face the facts and fight for breakthrough. The effort comes by consistent choices and a made-up mind to be an overcomer. Come in agreement with the work of Jesus on the cross, and see generational curses broken off of your life.

Overcome It

We discussed the importance of confronting the problem as well as facing it. With those steps in place, we must overcome it. Adam and Eve attempted to blame the problem away. Adam blamed God, and he blamed Eve. Then Eve then turned around and blamed the devil. Nothing is fixed or advanced by playing the blame game. If you are ready to come into agreement with Jesus and His finished work and shift the legacy of your family, then you must be an overcomer. This is the state in life when you became completely aware of the problems plaguing your family. You saw that your grandmother walked through the same issues as all the other women in your life. You choose not to sweep it under the rug and cover up the issues, but you confront it with actions—not confronting by blaming others for the state of life you are in but gaining the revelation that things can be different if you will be different. Thus, daily choices of picking up your cross and facing the giants in your family brought you to the fact that you are on the other end of the battlefield. You have bloody knuckles and scars across your body, but you fought through the mental battlefield. However, this is one of the hardest places to stay, people. Many around you will voluntarily or involuntarily pull you back into the cycle you just got out of. Nevertheless, you must remind yourself why you are fighting in the first place. You are fighting to overcome divorce, so your children will have a home with both Mom and Dad present. You are being an overcomer because you want to raise a family that finds joy without getting drunk or using drugs. You are being an overcomer because you are going to be the first person in your family to expand their education and go to college so that one day you will look at your children and say, If I can do it, then so can you." You are fighting the fight of your life to give, maintain, and excel in life. You are breaking the cycle. It is hard to stand at the other end of the battlefield because in order to get there, you have to walk past some bad influences. You had to mature past some bad behavior. The hard part about this place of victory is that others will say that you think you are better than they are or that you don't want to a part of the family. Don't believe those lies and get drawn into the cycle once again. All it takes is one person to jump off to break the rhythm. As you set an example for the ones around you, they will look at you and say, "Wow, I can have peace without drugs. I can have a healthy marriage with trust." The road to victory may be lonely at first, but soon you will have company. The fact of the matter is that Jesus already died to break the bondage of generational curses, yet by our own actions we lock ourselves up into that prison. However, for you and for your future's sake, you are leading the prison break. Sin entered the world because of a foolish choice. The wages of sin of the world was overcome by a priceless choice. Yet the benefit of that freedom is received from an intentional choice, a choice to confront rather than cover and face the issue rather than hide it. Finally, you made a choice to overcome rather than to blame. You are an overcomer, and you can shift the legacy of your family. As you dig your heels in the sand and refuse to be moved by the declining culture of our day and time, what will your children say thank you for? Will they say thank you for showing them what a healthy marriage looks like? Will they say thank you for going to college and showing them they can do it, too? Will they say thank you for cutting the cycle of alcoholism and showing them they can live a fun and a victorious life without a bottle? Will they say thank you for not smoking cigarettes to cope with stress but teaching them how to overcome it with healthy outlets and smarter choices? What will they thank you for? Resist the urge the quit. Will they say thank you for being an overcomer? Jesus acted as a thespian acting out the future of mankind to be the example to show us not to quit because the joy is on the other side of the pain. Joy isn't an emotion; it is a choice. Happiness is an emotion, but it is not joy. Happiness is directly correlated to a proper situation that demands happiness as the response. A birthday is a time of happiness, Christmas is a time of happiness. A buffet is a time of happiness—well, at least for me. Happiness needs your situation's permission to show up, but joy will make an appearance no matter what is going on. As Hebrews stated "For the joy set before him he endured the cross, scorning its shame." How could he possibly have joy at a time like that? Joy is not connected to a situation; Jesus's joy was connected to a cause. He saw past the pain of the cross and the torment of the crucifixion because He saw our faces. He is bridging the gap made by man and has reconciled them to Himself. Let the joy of the outcome of your effort help you to see past the pain connected to the process. Allow the joy of breaking generational curses be a cheerleader for you as you keep your legacy in mind. Remember why you fight, and keep fighting. Be an overcomer.

Galatians 6:9

Let us not become weary in doing good, for at the proper time we will reap a harvest if we do not give up.

You Shall Not Pass

A very famous series of books and movies called *The Lord of the Rings* illustrates the very truth of stepping up to the conflict that has changed families for generations. There is a scene when a team has been tasked with the burden of carrying a ring to the only place it could be destroyed. Along the way in this great journey, the darkness and all its minions are trying to overtake and overwhelm them. Wickedness is on the prowl to find the ring and bring chaos in the life of everyone in the world. Elves, humans, and dwarfs alike have all teamed up to combat this wickedness and unify themselves together for the greater good. One day, Frodo and his team of friends and warriors tasked in aiding him on the great endeavor found themselves chased by a large fiery monster. They ran as fast as they could to seek shelter and safety while a wise wizard who loved them dearly trailed behind. You could see the expression on Gandalf's (the wizard) face as the revelation sets in that if he doesn't turn around and face what has been chasing them, then all of them would die. They ran across a bridge hanging above a vast chasm when finally Frodo and the rest of the warriors make it safely to the other side. There in the middle of the bridge, Gandalf turned around and faced the whip and sword–wielding monster; with authority in his eyes and a love-driven conviction, he makes a stand. Raising his staff high in the air, he slams the end on the bridge while exclaiming these powerful words. "You shall not pass!" The bridge broke, and the monster and the fictional wizard fell along with it. Yet the fight wasn't over as he continued to wage war with the enemy until finally he was victorious.

When I think about breaking generational curses, this scene comes to mind: it is a person who loved this friends and family enough to stop running away from the problem but to confront it, face it and overcome it. I challenge you to face what has been trying to chase you down and sever the bridge of pain and actions connecting the issues from one generation to the other. The bridge is one that walked the problem from your great-grandmother to your grandmother to your mother and now is knocking at your door. It is not a bridge built with mortar and clay but of covering shame, hiding problems, and blaming issues. It is a bridge that is broken as you raise a standard though your actions, decreeing, "You shall not pass."

CHAPTER 8
FRAGILE, HANDLE WITH CARE

March 16, 2016, marked a moment in time that has changed my life forever. That wonderful day would grant me a gift that would keep on giving. That day was an instance in history that shifted my heart and expanded my understanding of unconditional love, a Wednesday in which my capacity to fathom even a glimpse of God's love for His children was bestowed on me. This monumental day was when I became a father. My amazing wife carried my son in her womb for the entire duration of the pregnancy and gave birth to an almost ten-pound baby boy. She was in labor for what felt like an eternity and pushed for four and a half hours. However, when she held the little miracle in her arms for the first time, no pain or inconvenience mattered. Joy overwhelmed the room as life was put into perspective at that moment. A sentiment of responsibility kept me company as I held my legacy in my hands.

People have been saying for years that the moment you become a parent, the understanding of God's love for you become greater appreciated, and it is a true statement. Many have asked me, "What was the initial thought and feeling you had when you held your son for the first time? Were you overwhelmed with love? Did you cry?" Even though these are suitable and proper reactions, this was not my experience. Crocodile tears didn't stream down my face to create a pool of happiness between my feet. Butterflies didn't take flight in my stomach. In my experience, it was as if time stood completely still, as if God himself grabbed the remote control used to regulate the broadcast of all reality and turned the volume down. I didn't hear the monotone rhythmic beeps of medical machines nor the chatter from the nearby nurses' station, enveloped in the epoch that lasted for a millisecond yet felt like an hour. Like a microscope studying the details of a cell, I zeroed into the face of my newly born son. I observed how he had my nose and my ears. He had my wife's skin tone as well as her eyes. I held him carefully as if a red label with white letters was inscribed on his clothing saying, "Fragile, handle with care." In that sobering moment, the very first thought I had was "How am I going to feed you?" Funny, I know, and for some it may seem out of order, but it was truly the first thought I had. Please don't be confused; love was present and kept me company the entire time, but responsibility opened the door and allowed love to come in.

Truly, the birth of my first-born son Hezekiah was a day that I will never forget. That moment was a physical experience, which communicated the reality of the love our heavenly Father has for us. My son is a gift from God, and his future is in God's hands, but his upbringing to that future is my wife's and my responsibility. The heart of a child is so delicate and demands daily devotion to the wellbeing of that miracle. God has granted us as parents with a calling to train up our children and raise them correctly. Being a parent is just that—a calling. Whether you helped give birth to the child or are the stepparent who stepped up to the plate, that calling is still there. We have to handle them with care. No logical person will take a box filled with fine china and glass cups and simply throw it around. It will be imprudent and absurd to place a box of books on top of the box with breakable glass. Why? Because you understand that it can't take the weight and that you have to handle it with care.

Voluntarily or involuntarily through the hardships of life, we as parents, coaches, mentors, and other voices can stack weights on the backs of children who are not strong enough to carry them. It is in times of anger, selfishness and other blinding emotions that some tend to lose sight of this truth. The integrity of a child's capacity to handle life situations is often overlooked as we place our worries on them. They then become the collateral damage of an internal war—POWs of an external battle and the hostages of emotional conflict. In the time that we are called to steward their precious lives, we can allow our pain to be our professor and seat them in the classroom of our crisis as they take notes gathered from the offense amassed in the shadow of grief. As the saying goes "hurt people hurt people." Our children are fragile, and we are called to handle them with care, not fragile regarding weakness, but fragile

> The integrity of a child's capacity to handle life situations is often overlooked as we place our worries on them. They then become the collateral damage of an internal war—POWs of an external battle and the hostages of emotional conflict

regarding importance. The greatest example of this is how our Father watches over us: "See what great love the Father has lavished on us, that we should be called children of God! And that is what we are! . . ." 1 John 3:1 New International Version (NIV)

Validity, Identity, and Affirmation

Born in humility and dying in victory, Jesus stunned the world. God entrusted the heroic task of raising the Son of God to parents named Joseph and Mary. Time went on as Jesus grew up and would soon start moving toward the purpose for which He was born. At the age of thirty, Jesus began His public ministry and for the next three and a half years, Jesus would turn this world upside down and inside out. Before He performed miracles that would amaze and impact the world, He was first baptized by a man named John the Baptist. John was a radical man, driven by a calling to persuade the importance of repentance. He was given the purpose to prepare a way for the Lord. Not a least bit fashionable, John wore clothes made out of camel's hair and wore a leader belt. He wasn't strutting down a runway like a model anytime soon. Preaching in a desert making the declaring to "Repent, for the kingdom of heaven is near," this man of God filled his stomach with wild honey. Saying that he was different from the average person around him would be an understatement to say the least. Yet, he like Jesus was given a task from heaven, and both were eager to fulfill the assignments. He knew of his heavenly task and nothing that anyone said would be able to stop Him.

Matthew 3:11

[11] "I baptize you with water for repentance. But after me comes one who is more powerful than I, whose sandals I am not worthy to carry. He will baptize you with[b] the Holy Spirit and fire."

The time arrived when the declaration from John's mouth would come to pass. Why? Because Jesus Christ would arrive at the waters of baptism. Jesus walked into the Jordan River and was baptized by John the Baptist.

Matthew 3:16–17

[16] As soon as Jesus was baptized, he went up out of the water. At that moment heaven was opened, and he saw the Spirit of God descending like a dove and alighting on him. [17] And a voice from heaven said, "This is my Son, whom I love; with him I am well pleased."

It's not the fact that Jesus needed this transaction from the heavenly Father, but it doesn't take away from the impact that just transpired. Jesus rose out of the stirred waters of the Jordan River to experience a powerful exchange. The Holy Spirit descended out of heaven like a dove. Along with that, a spotlight from the heavens was directed at Jesus, still dripping drops from his clothes back to the agitated water. In that open-heaven moment, God the Father spoke powerful words over and about His Son Jesus. "This is my Son, whom I love; with him I am well pleased." At that moment, publicly the Lord declared over His Son a truth that everyone in some capacity needs today. God gave Jesus validity, identity, and affirmation to whom He was and what He was called to do, validity in who He was and identified publicly what He was called to do. God also highlighted that fact that He is loved and God was well pleased. It's not the fact that Jesus needed it to do what He was called to do, but it is often what something people long for in our human form.

Just as the Lord did publicly to the Son of God, we also need to do for our children, who are gifts of God whom He entrusted us to raise. The Lord validated who Jesus was with simple yet powerful words "This is My Son." Jesus didn't have to roam the world wondering who He was or what His purpose was. He wasn't uprooted or derailed from the task because the distractions of life grabbed His attention. He didn't have to use life experiences as transactions to discover His purpose. He was born with a clear understanding of His orders from heaven. "This is My Son" and not only are you my son but also I love you and am well pleased with you.

The very encounter with God under that open heaven was put to the test when right after that Jesus was led into the desert for a time of prayer and fasting. After fasting for forty days, the same devil in the garden came to tempt Jesus. Armed with the same tactics that it used with Eve, that being half-truths and empty promises, he came to confront Jesus. Three times the deceiver tried to tempt Jesus. Twice, a direct statement that interrogated his very purpose by challenging him with instigated statements. "If you are the Son of God."

Matthew 4:2–11

² "After fasting forty days and forty nights, he was hungry. ³ The tempter came to him and said, "If you are the Son of God, tell these stones to become bread."

⁴ Jesus answered, "It is written: 'Man shall not live on bread alone, but on every word that comes from the mouth of God.'"

⁵ Then the devil took him to the holy city and had him stand on the highest point of the temple. ⁶ "If you are the Son of God," he said, "throw yourself down. For it is written:

"'He will command his angels concerning you, and they will lift you up in their hands, so that you will

not strike your foot against a stone.'"[7] Jesus answered
him, "It is also written: 'Do not put the Lord your
God to the test.' "[8] Again, the devil took him to a very
high mountain and showed him all the kingdoms of
the world and their splendor. [9] "All this I will give
you," he said, "if you will bow down and worship
me." [10] Jesus said to him, "Away from me, Satan! For
it is written: 'Worship the Lord your God, and serve
him only.'"[11] Then the devil left him, and angels came
and attended him"

Jesus never gave thought to the sly words of the accuser of the brethren.
"If you are the son of God," the enemy so boldly stated. Jesus just
had an encounter when the Father opened the heavens and declared,
"This is my son" Notice in the scripture that Jesus didn't go back and
forth debating with the enemy; He simply quoted what the word
of God said. He stated boldly words led by the endorsed statement
that was undergirded by the heavens "It is written"! If that were the
"TIV," the Timothy International Version translation of the conversation, it would read: "My Daddy said." Twice the enemy distorted
a statement that was diverse to Jesus's last experience under the open
heaven and the agitated baptism waters. The third and final time, the
enemy didn't question His identity nor His purpose yet attempted to
entice His motives. He was deceitful and promised that He will give
it all to Jesus if He bowed down and worshipped him. A significant
and imperative point is that the devil was trying to tempt Jesus with
things that were already His in the first place, trying to sway Him
with the very land and affirmation that He created with His words.
Yet Jesus never flinched, ended the conversation, and cast the enemy
out. Jesus knew who He was. He was very aware what He was called
to do and who called Him to do it. Jesus was afforded a mission to
fix the mistakes of man and nothing was going to stop or derail Him.

John 3:16–17

[16] "For God so loved the world that he gave his one
and only Son, that whoever believes in him shall not

perish but have eternal life. [17] For God did not send his Son into the world to condemn the world, but to save the world through him."

CPU

Many, due to a lack of identity, will place themselves on the clearance rack, believing a lie that they are less than everyone else. On a journey to discover who they are, they will engage in relationships with the hopes that someone else will tell them. They place a marker in the hands of strangers on social media or cycled boyfriends and girlfriends, asking them to fill out their nametag. "Hello, my name is (you fill in the blank)." Giving someone a price gun, as in a department store, and asking them to label their worth. Can you tell me who I am and tell him how much I am worth? When a person is at this state of mind, the distressed person will often use the very things most precious, as currency, to gain a watered-down form of gratification. They will use their heart as a checkbook and their purity as dollar bills. Trading the very thing that God commands us to protect to aid in fulfilling a void.

Proverbs 4:20–23

[20] My son, give attention to my words; Incline your ear to my sayings. [21] Do not let them depart from your eyes; Keep them in the midst of your heart; [22] For they are life to those who find them, And health to all their flesh. [23] Keep your heart with all diligence, For out of it spring the issues of life.

Our heart is the wellspring that is connected to many facets of life. It is connected to our thoughts, life, and interaction with others. It is intricately connected to our behavior, words, and actions in public and in private. Whatever is in you will influence what comes out of you. This is made overwhelmingly apparent when stress knocks on your door. When you are squeezed, you will find out what is in you, as Luke 6:45 states: "[45] A good man brings good things out of the good stored up in his heart, and an evil man brings evil things out of the evil stored up in his heart. For the mouth speaks what the heart is full of."

Our heart is the CPU of our lives, the central processing unit from which every instruction goes in and out. A computer monitor simply displays what is happening within the CPU, not the whole of the computer itself. It allows insight into what is being processed and presented. Monitors don't get viruses; the heart of the computer does. If there is a virus, then what is being seen will be affected by it. Does your central processing unit, your heart, have a Trojan horse virus that demands attention? If it is corrupt, then everything within it will be touched. Data will be distorted and in some areas, access to information will be denied. Often like when someone's heart is hurt, they cut off everyone and build up a wall to deny access. Passcodes won't work, and shortcut keys are made void. In that case, you will need to call someone who understands the idiosyncrasies of the CPU, the heart of the computer, a skilled professional that knows the ins and outs for the hardware and software. During times when the CPU of our heart has crashed, we need to give it over to God who is a trained professional, the one who knows your heart because He created it in the first place. The IT (informational technology) professional will ask you a simple and straightforward question, "What websites have you visited"? This question is important to ask because it is an indictor as to what baggage you picked up while you were there. What connected itself to you? What have you opened yourself up to by visiting or parked in the vulnerability of the information superhighway? It is unsecured places like this where identity theft happens, where your credit card information is taken or your social security number is stolen. It's identity theft, and the criminal wears many masks. It's malware of the heart, and it is after you. Malware is malicious software, such as a Trojan horse, that looks harmless but is filled with destruction. It is after innocently clicking on and or engaged that the true intent is revealed. Drama and problems flood out of the place of access. Our hearts so much like a CPU of a computer in that it is the wellspring of our lives that everything is connected to. The way we feel about ourselves and the way we treat others are swayed by our hearts, our actions, and engagement with others, manipulated by the predisposed state of our hearts. It is a well that many areas of life are drawn from; whatever drinks of its water will be either refreshed or poisoned. Who is drinking from your well? How are they served the water from your heart? Your spouse, children, and friends are some of the first to drink from your well due to the fact that they are the ones that have been given access. Are they being harmed by past memories or unforgiven transgressions? Are the children that resemble the ex-husband reaping the hurt of unchecked pain? Is the daughter being educated on value and self-worth by mimicking the risqué pictures you post to gain attention or likes? Are they drinking the residue of condemnation or actions left ignored rather than confronted?

Our well needs constant attention, not negligence. Imagine if you have two buckets of water, one being clean and the other dirty. If you take a teaspoon of clean water and pour it into the bucket of dirty water, nothing will happen to the water. It will simple blend itself in with the dirt by adopting its filth. However, if you take a teaspoon of dirty water and put it in bucket of clean water, the whole bucket of water will be affected. It then needs to be purified, boiled, and refined by fire. It needs a process, so when others drink from it, they will not be harmed. The wellspring of our hearts needs to be protected. It must be guarded because it's not a pain that solely affects you, but it greatly affects everyone connected to you. Sadly, as I said before, the very things worth posting guards to protect are the very things that we allow easy access to. No logical person would place armed security at the dumpsters of your local breakfast restaurant. Why? Because the trash isn't worth protecting. On the other hand, there is security in our banks, hospitals, governmental establishments, and hopefully our homes. Why? Because those things are worth protecting. Adam was given the command in the garden of Eden to subdue and guard the land, to protect his and his wife's place of residence. Yet overlooked or unseen was a deceiver resting on the branches of a tree no man should have touched. In that place, a simple question that is rehearsed in our generation today was asked of Eve. "Did God really say"? The enemy went on to tell her that she would be like God knowing good and evil. Falling into the trap of the enemy, Adam and Eve entertained the words of a snake, questioning who they are and who God told them they were, an action that would change the heart of man forever. Subdue and guard your land. Protect your heart because its actions will affect your generation to generations after you. Yet the very thing we are called to guard is the last thing surrounded by security. Parents, mentors, and leaders, we are called to help protect the hearts of our children. The enemy is on the prowl, and hearts are on his dinner menu, so aid in validating your children with the anticipation of ruining the devil's appetite. As the Lord had done in the day of Jesus's baptism, it is paramount that we bring validation, identification, and affirmation to our children.

Carousel

There is no such thing as a perfect parent because perfect people do not exist. Once again, this book is not intended to bash parents or wag a finger. It is intended to help raise a standard to create healthy families once again. It is intended to empower husbands to be the priests of their homes and subdue and guard their land. It is meant to encourage mothers to nurture a peaceful and healthy atmosphere with their words and action. It is aimed to cause attention to the difficult balance of gaining trophies, which is part of life, to make sure there is room and a place in your heart that others can rest under. For so long, family issues have been adopted as normal even though we all have them. Yet the problematic circumstance is not that problems exist because they are part of life; the issue is they are oftentimes not confronted in a heathy manner. They are gossiped about, Facebooked about, Instagramed about and tweeted about, but never in those methods is anything worked out. Don't lose sight of the crown of leadership that was placed on your heart and mind as you were anointed as parents and overseers. We have to lead and counsel in a healthy state. As stated many times hurt people will hurt people and sadly the children and spouse are oftentimes the ones tied up to the whipping post. There is not a healthy parent who would intentionally feed our children poison. However, oftentimes our unchecked pain is the liquid in the syringe of our words used, injected into the hearts of our offspring. Brokenness will give to brokenness until someone jumps off the carousel. I pray that the Holy Spirit has been keeping you company as you have been reading through these pages. Don't allow your pain to be a counselor. Don't allow offensive and indignant behavior to be the ungodly influence on your shoulder. Out of the abundance of the heart is a full spread of meals that many will sit at the table and eat. Make sure that it is a balanced meal rather than rotten offense. Remember the crown, remember the covenant and responsibility of a parent because the children are hanging on to and heeding our words.

Parental Poison

A mother who greatly failed in this endeavor was King Ahaziah's mother. Sadly, the word of God credits his very death and destructions to his mother, Athaliah.

> 2 Chronicles 22:2–4

> [2] Ahaziah was twenty-two years old when he became king, and he reigned in Jerusalem one year. His mother's name was Athaliah, a granddaughter of Omri. [3] He too followed the ways of the house of Ahab, for his mother encouraged him to act wickedly. [4] He did evil in the eyes of the Lord, as the house of Ahab had done, for after his father's death they became his advisers, to his undoing.

It is always appalling and alarming when you turn on the news or surf through the streams of social media to see that a parent would willingly cause harm to their own children. From mothers drowning their kids to fathers shooting up the entire family, it is a horrific tragedy. Stories that you read of parents providing drugs for their kids to sell or stories of parents pimping their own children on the streets as sex slaves, many of us will deem unacceptable these actions done to children, and rightly so. The question that we immediately ask is "How can a loving parent do such a thing?" No logical parent would do such a thing or even entertain the thought. Not only are these crimes done to kids horrific, so could be the apathetic spirit performing these actions that simply doesn't care.

Not caring enough who is connected or who influences the lives of this generation will only lead to pain and destructions. King Ahaziah's mother interactions in his life were not only unhealthy but also harmful. The counsel he received wasn't intended to keep him on a wholesome path. He was the head and the king, but she became his neck turning him to follow the ungodly and evil directions that she had on her agenda. Again, I know you as a reader, have been reading words like this and shaking your head in disgust. You love your children and the ones you are entrusted to lead, guide, and nurture. You would never even think about willingly leading your children astray. We will strive to do our very best to raise them correctly.

Proverbs 22:6

[6] "Train up a child in the way he should go, And when he is old he will not depart from it."

I am not so ignorant as to believe that all the problems in a child's life is because of a parent. You can raise two children exactly the same, and each one of them can come out different. One could be a great citizen and the other running the streets. Why? Because we all have free will. I know we, as imperfect people, would not willingly lead our families to their undoing. Yet knowingly or unknowingly, we're getting toxic results every day, not in the executions or radical violence we hear about on the news, but the killing of the emotional and spiritual wellbeing of families due to the counsel that hurt and flawed individuals give. It is oftentimes not intentional that we sow seeds of pain that will give birth to wickedness in the lives of our kids, but as the saying goes and been stated many times: hurt people hurt people.

Waving a flag

My wife and I travel as evangelists and have the great honor to see people saved and set free by the love of Jesus. We have also served as youth pastors for over a decade and believe strongly in this generation. We enjoy seeing the times that signs, wonders, and miracles take place in the services. From the times the people couldn't hear but God opened their ears or the ones that had no sight or simply had trouble seeing, the Holy Spirit invaded and ushered healing in their bodies. All of those encounters make me happy to see and encourages us not to give up and to keep living on faith and being obedient to the calling on our lives. Yet something that moves my heart every time I see it is when entire families get saved, or when they make a choice to serve the Lord in a deeper manner and confront the issues that are trying to nest in their family. We love seeing generational healing in the lives of everyday people. The heart of writing this chapter is not to wag the finger but wave a flag.

> The heart of writing this chapter is not to wag the finger but wave a flag.

We feel that due to the different exchanges, conversations, and encounters we have had in life that we have stepped into a role to give awareness to unsuspecting people. We are ambassadors, attempting to speak into the lives of loving parents that may be unaware of the pain their children are going though or even the pain they are unknowingly causing. On the other side of the coin, we are people standing in the gap for parents trying to reach their kids who are filled with entitlement and pride, unrelentingly chasing after the wrong things and running down a wrong path. We are people who want to help. So why am I giving this disclaimer? Because what you may read may seem hurtful or hard to swallow. Could you at times, through your own life crisis and unchecked pain, be giving the very children that we deeply love evil and ungodly counsel? Has the unforgiveness in your heart become so involved in your personality that you own the pain as part of your identity. The crime would be to think that topics like this is only directed to broken families, single parents, and children without a mom or dad actively involved. To think that would be a great error.

Don't skim though the last pages or move to the next chapter all the while hushing the cry of a generation pulling your coat tails down to gain your attention. The issues that are plaguing a family doesn't see color, class, or location.

Pain doesn't ignore the home centered in a gated community or the Section 8 place of residents in a dangerous part of town. Pain is pain, and it is often the loudest voice in the room even as it is whispering in silence. It is passed down through the words of sarcasm and derogatory statements that become a telltale sign that pain as been unchecked. It's the actions divorced parents display, such as talking about the child's father or mother like a dog or a deadbeat parent, with the impressionable children they are called to raise present and mindful. **It is extremely important to know that even though you have gotten divorced from your husband or wife, it doesn't mean your children are emotionally divorced from their mom and dad.** Pain and offense kicks down the doors of homes that have parents present but not engaged, and it is reaping havoc and taking no prisoners.

We have had countless of conversations with students around the nation, who are asking the same questions, going through the same anguish, and echoing pain. We have been given handwritten letters of heartbroken students wondering why their mother blames them for Dad leaving. We have received direct messages "DMs" though social media of kids, asking why my dad ignores me when I try to tell him about my problems. They keep saying that they are too busy or that they don't have enough time, only to see them moments later watching the playoff game. Drawing the conclusion that it wasn't the fact that they didn't have time, but it was that they didn't have time for them. We have been given countless numbers of razors and blades as students would cut themselves to find a moment of peace in a house of hardships, bearing the guilt of knowing that they were molested, yet believing the lie that they deserved it. Finally, we have been handed suicide letters of kids who wrote them out ahead of time before heading to camp or conventions. We will see them getting rocked by the presence of Jesus as we oftentimes minister on issues of the heart. They would tell us that they told God, "If You don't show me that You are real, then I am taking my life." Things like this are hard to read and swallow, but we must be ambassadors for a generation that truly believes that they are unwanted and unheard. The same sentence that was written on what seemed every letter, message, or email said, "If I would die or kill myself, my parents wouldn't even miss me." Allow that to sink in. What state of pain and confusion could a child be in to believe such a thing? What would draw them to think that they are unloved and unwanted? Yes, as parents, we work very hard to provide the necessities of life, such as food on the table, a roof over their heads, and clothes on their backs. Yet at the end of the day, they are the trophies that we gain in life that is vital for life. They aren't the banner that we wave to say, "Look what I am doing for you." No! They are our responsibilities that should happen in the first place. The trophies are needed, but they also need our crown. They are longing for our attention and time. Yet in the moments when they may try to talk, we tell them to get over it or it is not a big deal. I have way too many parents come into my office after a crisis with their kids, instead of the ones that notice and address the red flags. Our children are fragile. Though they may act tough, they are still fragile and need to be handled with care. Maybe these words have been empty, or have fallen on deaf ears, or simply overlooked because you may not believe it is applicable to your family and situation. If that is truly the case, then praise the lord and keep doing what you are doing. However, if you have noticed signs through the journey of these pages, then you need to take the next step, which is to ask them what is going on in their lives. Ask them if you have unwittingly said words to them that scarred them emotionally. Don't assume thing are okay because a smile at the dinner table could be faked even while a blade is run though their forearms, or while sending nude pictures and sexting to feel a sense of affirmation, no matter the transaction needed to get it. The drive to want to be wanted no matter the cost, posting a picture while angling the camera to emphasize certain physical features is done only to gain "likes" and thumbs up. Don't assume that issues like this can't happen in your home. I strongly encourage you to pull the rug out of your home and talk about the issues that are kicking down the door in the home.

Hold Your Ground

Don't allow the enemy to perch in the living room of your home, depositing lies to whomever walks by. Put on the full armor of God and make a stand. The battle can't be fought in silence but won with attention. Make your stand against the enemy's lies.

John 8:44 says, "When he lies, he speaks his native language, for he is a liar and the father of lies." The devil is the father of lies. Fathers are the ones who carry the seed. A father is someone who has sowed a seed or taken responsibility of a seed that has already been sown. So here is the key question: If the devil is the father of lies, then who is the mother? In order to be a father you have helped a mother to give birth; as the saying goes, it take two to tango. So if the devil is the father of lies, then who is the mother? If we are not careful, we are. We are the ones who adopt and receive the lies of the enemy in our lives. So where is the womb in which his demonic seed of lies is being nurtured? It is our minds; it is the place in which the umbilical cord is connected to feeding the lies and owning it as true. Take your stand against the enemy and wage war in the bloody battlefields of your mind. As *Ephesians 6:10 says, "¹⁰Finally, be strong in the Lord and in his mighty power. ¹¹ Put on the full armor of God, so that you can take your stand against the devil's schemes."*

I read the verse in Ephesians 6:10 wrong for most of my life. I read it as it saying, "so that you can take your stand against the devil's lies." However, that is not what Paul said when writing to the church of Ephesus. He told them to take their stand against the devil's schemes. This is deeper than a lie; this is a plan. We must take our stand against the father of lies' plans, the very brick it is built by is made of lies and half-truths. Not only does God have a plan for your life, but the enemy does also. The devil isn't God's equal and he doesn't know the future. He is not Alpha and Omega, the beginning and the end. God knows our tomorrow while it still was yesterday. The enemy can only seize the day through the doors we open for him. Yet he still has a plan—a plan to rob, kill, and destroy you. The enemy recognizes our seed as he is on a mission to uproot it before its roots can find the waters of hope. His sole purpose is to abolish the plan that God has for you and your family. Put on the full armor of God and make a stand. Stand for your children's peace. Stand for the health in your family and hold your ground. Dig your heels in the dirt and take a stand. When the great armies of old were lined up for battle, the general would yell simple words as the enemy charges toward them. He would yell, *"Hold your ground."* I pray that those simple words will echo in your heart as you fight on behalf of your family. Hold your ground.

CHAPTER 9
ONLY GOD CAN JUDGE ME

The wall that was elevated in the hearts of the kings in the book of Chronicles was entitlement. The rebar that strengthens its integrity was pride. Entitlement and pride are a couple that can't be separated. They are always with each other. These ideologies are quickly endorsed and defended to keep. War is waged as boulders inscribed with "You're just a hater" are hurled from the catapult of their mouth from the bird nest of their castles. Its seems impossible to aid in the direction of someone's life while they are listening to the symphony of pride through the noise-canceling headphones of entitlement, attempting to drown out ill-wanted voices even if it's the guidance they need. So how do you help and lead someone who thinks they don't need to be led? How do you raise kids who truly believe they know it all? How do you "handle the teenager with care" when they disregard the voice of direction you give? It is an uphill battle and fight that can be exhausting. Entitlement is a grenade with the pin pulled. It is only a matter of time until it destroys something.

> Entitlement is a grenade with the pin pulled. It is only a matter of time until it destroys something.

The strenuous efforts prophets made, pleading for the kings to repent were rejected as pride had their ear, and entitlement seized their attention. All three generations of kings failed at the end of their lives because of the same internal conflict. It wasn't addressed; it was simply accepted. They went out of their way to uphold their own agenda and even, at times, violently opposed the voices of reason in their lives. King Joash, after the death of Priest Jehoiada, abandoned the temple of God and started to worship idol gods. Who knows what was going through his mind, but any loving and concerned person who had access into his life wouldn't stay silent but attempt to recalculate his route. Pride and entitlement being the puppeteer pulling the strings of his heart blinded them to think that the wrongs were right and the rights are wrong; that the standards that God set, for whatever reason, didn't apply to him. As the kings were crowned, they were also given a copy of the covenant, so the excuses of not knowing God's thoughts about this issue are out of the question. King Joash even ordered the Prophet Zechariah, the son of the Priest Jehoiada, killed.

2 Chronicles 24:19–22

[19] Although the Lord sent prophets to the people to bring them back to him, and though they testified against them, they would not listen. [20] Then the Spirit of God came on Zechariah son of Jehoiada the priest. He stood before the people and said, "This is what God says: 'Why do you disobey the Lord's commands? You will not prosper. Because you have forsaken the Lord, he has forsaken you.'" [21] But they plotted against him, and by order of the king they stoned him to death in the courtyard of the Lord's temple. [22] King Joash did not remember the kindness Zechariah's father Jehoiada had shown him but killed his son, who said as he lay dying, "May the Lord see this and call you to account.'"

He took a drastic exploit taken against Zechariah, all because Zechariah loved and cared about him enough to tell him the truth. As the saying goes, the truth hurts; people will go to great extents not to hear it. Pride became the nails that sealed King Joash's coffin. After the atrocious and horrendous crime toward the Lord and to the prophet, his obituary was being written by the very people who he once led in greatness. At that moment, none of the trophies and accomplishments mattered. At the same time that King Joash invested in repairing the temple of God, he had allowed his temple within to fall apart. His spiritual real estate was in foreclosure. King Joash was murdered in his bed. Entitlement and pride are blinders willingly worn while prancing toward a cliff without guardrails. Like a family heirloom, the behavior was simply passed down to another generation. King Amaziah would sit on the same throne, and he would be dethroned by the same issues of entitlement and pride as his father before him. From an advancement and building aspect, King Amaziah, along with his father, knocked it out of the park. They could lead at times, but they just didn't live well. The king went on a siege and conquered a land, yet just like his father, started to worship idols. It wasn't like he had no idea what happened to his father. What could have had such a hold on his moral compass for him to truly believe that this was a positive direction? Why would he believe the covenant that he promised to uphold when he was crowned as king didn't apply to him? This is one of the many dangers of entitlement and pride. It is the concreate internal fortitude that the rules don't apply to you and that you earned the right to supersede them and avoid its consequences. Yet King Amaziah, just as his father, was greatly mistaken.

2 Chronicles 25:14–16

[14] "He brought back the gods of the people of Seir. He set them up as his own gods, bowed down to them and burned sacrifices to them. [15] The anger of the Lord burned against Amaziah, and he sent a prophet to him, who said, "Why do you consult this people's gods, which could not save their own people from your hand?" [16] While he was still speaking, the king said to him, "Have we appointed you an adviser to the king? Stop! Why be struck down?" So the prophet stopped but said, "I know that God has determined to destroy you, because you have done this and have not listened to my counsel."

Only God Can Judge Me

King Amaziah collected the idols from his siege and worshipped the very things he had defeated. Feeling like a god in his own mind and electing to ignore the commands of the one true God, just as his own dad had, he rejected the ones who cared about him enough to confront him with the truth. You can't be mad at the doctor because the needle hurts, even though the antidote will resolve the issue. Yet, he slapped away the prophet attempting to administer truth to a king entangled in pride.

Pay close attention to the interaction between the prophet and the fallen king. While the incense was burning for the false god, the prophet, being the mouthpiece of God here on earth, confronted him with a mission for him to stop and get back on track. The prophet, that God has ordained to speak through, was sent to him to pull him out of the quicksand of entitlement. Yet while he was mid-sentence, the king interrupted him. I can picture the prophet passionately pleading with King Amaziah, when abruptly the conceited man puts a hand up with his palm facing out in the face of the prophet, rolls his neck, pulls his head back, and smacks his lips. Speaking in a derogatory and condescending tone ask, *"Have we appointed you an adviser to the king? Stop! Why be struck down?"* It is as if you can feel the tension as you read this altercation in the word of God. Who does prophet God thinks he is? Does he know who I am? I am the king, and I can do whatever I want to do. I sit on the throne. After all I've done for you, do you think I deserve this? Could these be the thoughts that raced through the mind of the king? Conversations like this happen every day.

This dialogue occurs when a person believes that everyone who speaks to them with the drive to help them is only there to hate on them. They hold a false notion that attention is the same as altercation, and in order to remove the chance to be confronted, they will make a statement completely taken out of context to foolishly hinder the integrity of the intent behind the discussion. The misguided person will say, "Only God can judge me," using this phrase to push away words that are touching on erroneously adopted action. "Only God can judge me" is a phrase that I grew up hearing. You can see it on social media where people complete "about me" on their profile. It is printed out on shirts and tattooed on the skins of the misinformed. It sounds like scripture, but it is pulled out of context, thus creating a manufactured truth that was never the Lord's. The devil did the same thing to Eve and attempted to do it to Jesus, using the word of God out of context to achieve his own results. Sadly, whether on purpose or by mistake, we are modeling after that behavior and distorting the Word of God for our own personal gain. Disclaimer: by no means am I saying that you are the Holy Spirit policemen or that you're judge and executioner. We aren't the Judge Dreed of our society but that doesn't mean that we are to refrain from being honest with each other. However, pointing out an issue without leading them to the solution, which is Jesus, is pointless. Showing the disease of sin without leading them to the medication isn't an act of love. The conversations need to lead them to Jesus.

Luke 6:37–42

37 ""Do not judge, and you will not be judged. Do not condemn, and you will not be condemned. Forgive, and you will be forgiven. 38 Give, and it will be given to you. A good measure, pressed down, shaken together and running over, will be poured into your lap. For with the measure you use, it will be measured to you."39 He also told them this parable: "Can the blind lead the blind? Will they not both fall into a pit? 40 The student is not above the teacher, but everyone who is fully trained will be like their teacher.41 "Why do you look at the speck of sawdust in your brother's eye and pay no attention to the plank in your own eye? 42 How can you say to your brother, 'Brother, let me take the speck out of your eye,' when you your-self fail to see the plank in your own eye? You hyp-ocrite, first take the plank out of your eye, and then

you will see clearly to remove the speck from your brother's eye."

The blunder transpires if you stop reading the entire passage of scripture after the first nine words. Take the scenic route though this passage to discover the purpose behind the words of Jesus. Verses 37 and 38 are deliberating about the law of sowing and reaping, an understanding that whatever seed you sow you will gain back in a greater measure. If I plant an apple seed in fertile soil, I don't expect only one apple to grow. However, an understanding is made that I can expect many apples to be created from that one action of sowing. Whatever we sow will be returned back to us whether that seed is good or whether that seed is bad. That is one of the many reasons why we need to give strong thought to what we are doing and saying; we are all farmers wielding our actions as the mule preparing the ground for a harvest. Thus, if you are sowing forgiveness, then you can expect forgiveness to be returned back to you—maybe not by the person you are casting the seeds toward but forgiveness nonetheless. If you are sowing discord, you can take it to the bank that drama will soon follow you. Whatever you give, the act of giving is returned back to you. Jesus is simply talking about the law of sowing and reaping. Therefore, if you are going to sow seeds of viewing the fruit of someone else's life, then you need to be prepared that the same judgment and attention is heading your way. I believe that error is made because we view the word *judge* as the person who sends an individual to their condemnation. The person that is being condemned then thinks, *Who are they to send me to my punishment when they have crimes of their own?* As believers, we can't send anyone to their condemnation; they do that themselves. We are called to be lighthouses that shine brightly into the dark abyss, so unknowing ships don't crash on the unseen rocks of the shore of life. A flashlight needs to be pointed in the direction of the dark area in order to give guidance and attention. However, we have been so brainwashed by a statement taken out of context that we have willingly turned off our lights with the hope of not being labeled as someone who judges. All the while, a friend is cutting himself or herself at night and is addicted to

Love is an action, not an excuse.

prescription drugs, killing themselves. Yet the greatest act of love is to be silent rather than say anything. No! That would be foolish. Love is an action, not an excuse. Jesus clarifies and breaks down his statement in verse 37 about judging with an illustration. It's critical that you pay attention to the words that Jesus chooses to use. He tells a parable and asks the question of why you are attempting to remove the "speck of sawdust" from your brother's eye and not paying attention to the "plank" in your own eye. We need to make sure that we are evaluating the fruit of our own lives as we aid in helping someone else. This is not the excuse to hang our hat of effort on. This is also not saying that we have to be perfect before we address matters that may be harming our loved ones, friends, and strangers.

> Perfection was never the prerequisite to say anything or to act. Rather the criteria is love and self-evaluation

Perfection was never the prerequisite to say anything or to act. Rather the criteria is love and self-evaluation. If perfection were the requirement to be a Christian than none of us would be qualified to be one. Are you doing it in love? Have you searched your own lives? What are our motives to address the issues in the first place? Are we only doing so to pull the person down? Are we only addressing the situation to have ammunition to gossip about the other person because they sin differently than you? Is there a legitimate concern about the physical, mental, emotional, and spiritual wellbeing of the other individual? Jesus elucidates and expounds on the unseen truth that entitlement and pride attempts to blind one from seeing. Pay close attention to the instructions that Jesus articulates in this often-misunderstood passage of scripture. "*First* take the plank out of your eye, *then* you will see clearly to remove the speck from your brothers' eye." Jesus never said not to give attention to the issue in the other person's eye. However, we are to make sure that the foremost action is to remove and evaluate the hindrance in our own life. It is with these actions that we can healthy and fittingly give consideration and aid to the other person. *This isn't a cross-measuring contest but a drive to aid each other toward Christ and an overcoming life.* Don't be like the king and stop the voice of God through the prophet when he asked, "What gives you the right to speak to me? Are you my advisor?" Again, if this were the "Timothy International Version" it would say, "Who are you to tell me what to do? You ain't my daddy!"

Hell is very real as well as heaven. In addition to the destination of one's afterlife, our choices affect us while we are still walking the earth. We should have motivation to speak with love to someone who is walking with a blindfold toward destruction instead of saying we love the person and still stay silent. The enemy loves and oftentimes resides in silence, and we pay his lease in our homes by not addressing issues.

> Romans 10:14
>
> "How, then, can they call on the one they have not believed in? And how can they believe in the one of whom they have not heard? And how can they hear without someone preaching to them?"

CHECK, CALL, CARE

When I was in high school in Eden, North Carolina, I wanted to go into the medical field. One of the classes I chose to join was a health class called Health Occupations Students of America. I had an amazing and passionate teacher named Mrs. Martha. She was one of the examples of someone who would go over and beyond to help people. She displayed a characteristic of servanthood and compassion that I decided to model in my life, and she quickly became my favorite teacher. I grew up in poverty, and she didn't turn a blind eye to my situation. On one of my birthdays, she took me out with the class to eat at the New Mexican restaurant in town. To this day, I still remember what I ordered—chicken nachos baptized in cheese. I was in heaven and savored every bite. Mrs. Martha also helped me get a tuxedo for my prom, so I could go. Back then, I really didn't believe in myself and as I look back, it is encouraging to know that others

> The enemy loves and oftentimes resides in silence, and we pay his lease in our homes by not addressing issues.

believed in me. In that class, we learned about the medical field and trained in the local hospitals and rehabilitation centers.

At the end of the class, I took the state test and received my Certified Nurse Assistant License. I used what I learned and worked as a CNA throughout my time at Bible school where I attended the North Carolina Masters Commission at the time to aid in paying for my tuition. During those times at the rehab center during the lunch break, we would have Bible studies and powerful prayer gatherings. Plenty of times people were slayed in the Holy Spirit and getting saved right there during our break. We saw Jesus move and revival stirring in that place. A lesson that I learned during the teenage years from my health class was about responding to crisis. What do you do if you come up to a car accident and someone is in need of assistance or if someone is injured? What are the proper steps to take to make sure the person received the best and quickest medical treatment possible? The steps that I retained are the three "Cs": check, call, and then care. You're driving down Interstate 4 in central Florida when all of a sudden the car in front of you has a tire blowout. The vehicle swerves back and forth, attempting regain control when it hits a guardrail and then stops. According to step one, you need to check the situation out and make sure that it is safe for you to go to the person in need. After all, if you are hit by a car in traffic, then you will be zero help. Once you deem it as safe to approach the injured person then you will check on their current state. Is there gasoline leaking out of the car? Is there a fire? Is the person conscious or in shock? All of this is happening in seconds as you gather enough information to complete the next step, which is to call. We have all seen the movies where a panicked person comes to an accident and yells to the crowd, "Someone call 911!" This is an incorrect action to take. The proper step is that someone needs to be pointed out to call 911. "*You* call 911." The reason is that many will think, as bystanders, that someone else already called 911, so they will not make the call. That raises the chance that no one will be called at all. Someone needs to be pointed out and burdened with the responsibility to make the call, along with the information that you received from step one, which is to check. Finally, we have to care. After you checked the situation and the circumstance of the injured person and you know that 911 has been called, then you administer care. Whether it is safely pulling them out of the car, administering CPR, or giving first aid, you are putting actions to what you observed. You keep giving care until the ambulance arrives. Again, this is not a long, drawn-out process; in fact, all of this can happen in seconds. Three simple steps to remember during a complicated moment in crisis are to check, call, and care.

Heroic people, both with and without a badge, step up to help others in need. Why? Because they know that death and life hangs in the balance. They are suddenly driven with a cause to push away their schedule, agenda, and placing themselves on the need to help, at times, complete strangers. What an incredible picture of humanity. What drives the middle-aged man to pull over to the help the senior citizen change a tire or help load grocery bags in their car on a rainy day? What drives a complete stranger to pull out their jumper cables to jump the car of someone they don't know? What fuels a firefighter to run into an engulf building covered in flames to save unfamiliar people? One word can boil down all the heroic and innate instinct that many of mankind possesses, one word that even is used to describe the work of Jesus: this word is compassion.

Matthew 20:34 International Standard Version (ISV).

> "Then Jesus, deeply moved with compassion, touched their eyes, and at once they could see again. So they followed him."

The example of our Lord and Savior Jesus Christ boils down the heart of evangelism and the mission statement of a Christian. Compassion must be in our lives if we have any appeal to reach the lost, broken, and forgotten. We're called not only to reach the down and out but also the up and over. All of us need Jesus in our lives, and we are the hands and feet of the kingdom to exercise this truth. We must check, call, and care in our families, communities, nation, and the world. Yet the enemy to compassion is apathy. It will smother out a fire, turn off a light, and siphon out the fuel required to act. Cultivating a lethargic and complacent spirit in the breeding ground of taciturnity and indifference aids in creating a self-inflicted excuse that answering the call isn't our responsibility. Yet that couldn't be further from the truth. We must aid in our world caught in tragedy and imprisoned hopelessness. We must discard the mindset that it is none of my business, so why would I help the bleeding person on the side of the road or the recently divorced family in my neighborhood. We must be like Jesus and be a light, thus shining hope in dark and lost times. Let your light shine by stepping into the void of someone else's hopelessness and directing them toward the Hope, which is Jesus.

Let There Be Light

Genesis 1:3

"And God said, "Let there be light," and there was light."

At the inception of creation, God said, "Let there be light." Light was painted on the canvas, which was once formless and empty; light appeared, thrusting into existence at an incredible speed of 299,792,458 meters per second from the paintbrush of His words. A distinct and visual separation for darkness and day appeared. Times went on, and Jesus walked the earth, doing the works of God. John, chapter 8, opens up with an amazing act of love and compassion. It is a story in which Jesus stepped in the gap for a woman caught in the act of adultery. The Pharisees dragged her in front of Jesus, attempting to trap Jesus. By law, she was supposed to be stoned to death. However, the giver of life was standing up for life and did in fact save her life. He bent down and wrote on the dirt not saying a word. Bewilderment must have struck the religious people, wondering why He was doing what He was doing. Finally, Jesus says, "Let any one of you that is without sin cast the first stone." As we read in a previous chapter, Jesus stood in the gap for her. One by one, the tightly clenched hands of the eager Pharisees released the archaic bullet. Stones would hit the ground echoing grace rather than death. In the aftermath of this moving passage of scripture and testimony, the Son of God affirms this statement: *"I am the light of the world. Whoever follows me will never walk in darkness, but will have the light of life"* John 8:12

The fruit that Jesus bore in three and a half years of ministry gave validity to His declaration. Jesus brought light, and thus life went wherever He went. Just as trees in a rainforest would bend and grow to perch under the rays of light, so should our lives be, absorbing the light of Christ as an act of spiritual photosynthesis, converting the light of love that we greatly receive and transferring it into actions that our world truly needs. While our society is suffocating in despair, we process the love we received from the light and life of Jesus to bestow the oxygen they need to breathe. So many are dead men walking, yet we are called to transfer the light of life. This was clear to Jesus when He spoke to the disciples about their light.

Matthew 5:14–16

""You are the light of the world. A town built on a hill cannot be hidden. ¹⁵ Neither do people light a lamp and put it under a bowl. Instead they put it on its stand, and it gives light to everyone in the house. ¹⁶ In the same way, let your light shine before others, that they may see your good deeds and glorify your Father in heaven."

Everyone's life preaches a sermon. Our actions and fruit are the illustrated message, which authenticates the words that come out of our mouths or what we shout about on Sunday mornings. Either God or the enemy will step behind the pulpit of our hearts and deliver the altar call. Who are we welcoming as the speaker? This is determined by how we are living our life, the fruit we bear, and our deeds. So the question to pounder is, who will respond to the altar call? Are we living a life preaching that Jesus isn't vital or important, or are we preaching an action-oriented gospel, saying that we are all imperfect people chasing after a perfect God who perfects us? As the saying goes, "Actions speak louder than words." We must allow our light to shine. When I was a little boy, I remember receiving a great gift, plastic planets and stars that you stick on the celling and they glowed in the dark. I thought it was the coolest thing in the world. When I opened the package, it came with clear instructions. If these instructions weren't followed, then the product would not be used for its intended purpose. The directives were to hold the plants and stars to a light for an extended period of time. Once they've had enough exposure to the light, it will absorb the rays. I could tell that is worked because the moment that the lights were turned off, it emitted a greenish light. It literally glowed in the dark. As Christians, we must do the same thing. We must glow in the dark. Our actions and deeds must be proof that we have spent time under the light, which is the "*Son*," and release light in return.

God said "Let there be light," Jesus said "I am the light of the world." He then gave us the command: "Let you light shine among men." Our light is important, and we can't put the lamp under a bowl any longer. Yet when we refuse to open our mouth in love to a person in need because we don't want to be labeled as someone who judges, we flip the switch off on our spiritual flashlights. Flashlights are most effective when it is dark, so why are we turning ours off. Before God said, "Let there be light," there was complete darkness. My scientist believes that darkness in itself isn't real, yet it is just the default of light. When you turn a light switch on, light appears, but when you switch it off it leaves. Darkness never leaves; it is always there, but in order for darkness to be forced out, light must make an appearance. What if there is so much darkness running rampant in the world today because we as Christians are refusing to show up, declining to open our mouths in sincere love and concern because the fear of being branded as someone who judges?

If we are going to see any transformation, revival, or awakening in our world today, then the church can no longer be silent but active. Again, with the attempt to bring clarification to the ones reading that has already taken out your Holy Ghost belt on a mission to put everyone over your knee of a spiritual spanking. Remember that this is not a command to be mean, rude, and forgetful of God's grace, but a plea to know that we have permission from God to walk with our brothers and sisters in life. At times that is to encourage, and at other moments it may mean we must correct. The enemy dwells in silence and adores a silent Christian. Silence is the red carpet that welcomes the enemy in far too many families. It's the rug that crisis is swept under and the closet that emotional trauma is compartmentalized. Open your mouth; it is healthy to talk about what is going on. Break the generational curses over you and against your family. We have dulled our swords in apathy while trying to cut the chains of indifference.

> Silence is the red carpet that welcomes the enemy in far too many families. It's the rug that crisis is swept under and the closet that emotional trauma is compartmentalized.

2 Timothy 4:2

"Preach the word; be prepared in season and out of season; correct, rebuke and encourage—with great patience and careful instruction."

"Preach the Word!" Share the heart of Jesus that was written out to us in His word. So many long to hear His voice, which is amazing. Yet even at times when you can't hear His voice, you can always read His words. Even though you may not hear the phone call, you can always open up the text message. If your friend is swaying from the path and not seeing the red flags along the way, love them enough to gain their attention. "Hey! I love you enough to tell you that I am concerned about the path you are starting to take." Be bold enough, yet loving enough, to tell your sister who is sleeping around to find love that there is a better way. Tell her that the void she is trying to fill because of the emptiness within isn't going to be satiated with one-night stands and empty beer bottles. Reassure them that they can be an overcomer. Remind them they aren't walking through the challenging season alone. It's not enough to solely call out an issue, but we must aid in helping them overcome it. Again, we are all taking the journey of life together and different issues cause's various people to slip and fall. Maybe you are standing in victory over an issue that they just fell over from. Don't stand above them with an elevated chin and a puffed-out chest, thinking that you are better. No!

Stretch out your arm and give them a hand up. Educate and teach them how you have learned to say no to the desires and what practical steps you take. Maybe it isn't walking down the aisle at the grocery store that sells beer. Maybe you refrain from using your phone late at night with the concern of being overwhelmed by temptation. Whatever it may be, be an aid not a hindrance.

Bounty Hunters and Nurses

We aren't called to be Holy Spirit bounty hunters, but we are called to be Holy Spirit Nurses. We don't arrest someone because of the fruit and then condemn them to die by our own standards all the while gossiping about how Sue did such and such and how you would never do such a thing. Conversations like that simply give evidence to the pride that may be hidden and attempting to show its revolting head. When we talk down to people who struggle differently than us; we attempt to make them the armrest in our figurative chair. When you are sitting down on a chair, you push down on the armrest to help with standing up, thus pushing down on things to elevate yourself. Stop using others whose mistakes are different from yours to elevate ego. Judging other by their fruit doesn't mean to condemn but simply means to confront. Notice the example when Jesus, in Luke 6, told the man that when he removed the plank out of his own eye, only then would he see clearly to speak of sawdust from his brother's eye. Yet how could he aid in removing the speck if it is unbiblical to notice it in the first place? The fruit of our actions will bring consequences with it. Penalties for unethical behavior are going to happen, and they don't need the aid of a masquerading Christian to condemn them to it. We are lovingly confronting the speck in our brothers and sisters eye because we are very aware of the penalties. It's the concern that should drive us to act as nurses, not as God's bounty hunters. Our Lord and Savior led the charge not only in His life but also in His death.

> We aren't called to be Holy Spirit bounty hunters, but we are called to be Holy Spirit Nurses.

John 3:16–17

"For God so loved the world that he gave his one and only Son, that whoever believes in him shall not perish but have eternal life. [17] For God did not send his Son into the world to condemn the world, but to save the world through him."

Jesus judged the world by their fruit and knew that He had to act. He didn't come to condemn because condemnation was the end result if He didn't come in the first place.

Romans 6:23

"For the wages of sin is death, but the gift of God is eternal life in Christ Jesus our Lord."

He didn't come as a bounty hunter but as a doctor being the remedy to the disease of sin infesting mankind. He is the Great Physician, beckoning people into the hospital of His presence where they can receive whatever is needed to gain health, hope, forgiveness, freedom, or whatever they need. You will never walk into the doctor's office without being asked what is wrong. The nurses or people at the front desk will give you paperwork to be filled out and will certainly ask the question "Why do you need to see the doctor today?" In order to receive the aid needed, the question must be answered honestly. Yet how can you answer the question honestly, if you can't judge the fruit of your life. We as Christians are not the Great Physicians, but we are called to be His nurses, aiding others to get to a place in their life where they will receive the help and aid from the doctor. We can have malpractice in our faith by staying silent and watching our patients die in an issue that we ignored. True love is vocal but not necessarily confrontational. Yet if conflict of an issue finally arises because love was administered, take them to see the doctor. Respond to the emergency until the medical professional help arrives.

CPR

Previously, we talked about how to respond to a life-and-death emergency. The three steps to take are check, call, and care. Check and assess the situations so you can see how to navigate though it appropriately, checking to see if it is safe for you to approach the accident. Check to see the state of the victims. After checking, the next step to take is to call. Point out someone nearby and assign them to responsibility to call 911. If no one else is present, the obligation falls on you to make the call. Finally, after you checked and called, now it is time to give the care. During this time, maybe you discovered that they aren't breathing, and they are in need of CPR.

"Cardiopulmonary Resuscitation (CPR)" is an technique that uses chest compressions with artificial ventilation to preserve brain function and to keep the blood circulating and the person breathing. The compressions on the heart attempting to manually keep blood pumping and the air are aiding to keep brain function. You keep doing CPR until they are resuscitated or until professional medical help arrives.

We live in a society that is in cardiac arrest. No longer, can we sit silent and watch families, loved ones, and the world in general die from issues of the heart. Don't sit at your dinner table, watching your family spiritually pass away and stay silent. Don't aid your friend who's cutting himself or herself by not trying to get them the help they need. Don't sit silent because of offense and hand your marriage to the enemy. The issue is of the heart, and it is time for CPR. Judge the moment, see the fruit, and respond. As you remove the plank from your eye and give attention to the speck in your brother and sisters, give CPR. Respond to the dying heart with compressions of love and grace and air of hope and peace. Give and pray for spiritual CPR, not cardiopulmonary resuscitation, but *conviction, prayer, and repentance.*

> Respond to the dying heart with compressions of love and grace and air of hope and peace. Give and pray for spiritual CPR, not cardiopulmonary resuscitation, but conviction, prayer, and repentance.

Conviction, Prayer, and Repentance

Intercede so that as you are helping with the issues of the heart, they will heed to the conviction that God operates in. Being vocal yet loving isn't an act of hate but an act of love. Jesus loved us enough to shine light into the area that is separating us from Him. It's not as simple as wagging a finger that is going to make someone change. Nagging isn't going to resolve the issues, either. Pray and live a life that reflects the Jesus that you are preaching. Only the Holy Spirit is going to bring you to a place where change is discovered.

Psalm 139:23–24

"Search me, God, and know my heart; test me and
know my anxious thoughts.
24 See if there is any offensive way in me, and lead
me in the way everlasting."

Pray for God's strength to overcome the stronghold that has been keeping them bound. God will walk with them every step of the way. Pray for the drive to act out what God is revealing to them. Pray that they evaluate the relationships and choices in their life—which ones are healthy and which ones are toxic. Finally, repentance is vital. The misconception of repentance is that it is simply a "sorry." That is far from the truth. Repentance is to apologize yet with the intent to change. Repentance is to change directions, not to continue on the path but sorry you were caught. Pray that as you are administrating spiritual CPR, that change and life will happen once again.

The legacy and life of Kings Joash, Amaziah and Uzziah would have been so different if they would have taken hold of this. Rather in the times that they could have repented and changed directions, they argued and beat their chest, fighting for entitlement, caressing ego, and removing any voice that would tell them any different. Take control of your family and talk about issues, rather than ignoring them. Be willing to be respectfully approached and fight the giants of indifference together. Drown out silence or the whispers of pride with the shouts of love and grace.

CHAPTER 10

CULTIVATING A SERVANT'S HEART

Matthew 20:28

"just as the Son of Man did not come to be served, but to serve, and to give his life as a ransom for many."

No greater model of exhibiting a servant's heart has ever walked this earth than our Lord and Savior Jesus Christ. He marched through society mandated with a mission, a task that in itself carried a vision that was beyond His own wellbeing. As I am writing this book, it is a few days away from Christmas, a great reminder that even while He was wrapped in swaddling clothes laying in a manger that He had a mission in mind. He had a drive to serve mankind with His life and death to reconnect us back to the Father. Jesus went around healing the sick, restoring lives, and raising the dead. He is our greatest example of servanthood. God did whatever he needed to do to make sure his children were taken care of. The peak of this truth was when He carried a heavy rugged cross to the place of his execution. There He willingly gave everything to us. He served his death, not on a platter, but on a cross, so all mankind would have the opportunity to partake of its benefits. He is the pinnacle of faith, sacrifice, and servanthood for all of us. Yet he didn't serve to do it for us but to show

> He served his death, not on a platter, but on a cross, so all mankind would have the opportunity to partake of its benefits. He is the pinnacle of faith, sacrifice, and servanthood for all of us

us how to do it. We must cultivate a servant's heart as our exemplar, not simply to talk about it but to bear its fruit. As the Holy Spirit dwells in the lives of every believer, we must show evidence to that effect. God started man in a garden, around agriculture, and with the task to tend to it. In that equivalent manner, we must look after the fruits and seeds planted in the figurative garden of our own lives. Find a green thumb and reap the harvest of servanthood. As Christians, Christ-like people, we must mimic the greatest servant of all, our Savior Jesus Christ. As I travel the world preaching the gospel, I am convinced of this daunting truth; many people in this world believe that Jesus is real and that He exists. The predicament is that they just don't believe the ones representing him. *When we lost sight of the cross, we lose sight of its mission.* That is to serve the world with the great commission, driven in a vehicle of love and grace. *"By this everyone will know that you are my disciples, if you love one another.""* John 13:35

Sign Language

Many in our society today believe that the word of God is solely a history and storybook. Some will categorize the Bible as fictional and archive it next to the *Chronicles of Narnia*. Whether through letdown, crisis, or church hurts, some people drew the conclusion that God isn't real. If you attempt to converse with them and encourage them with the Word, your efforts will have the same nostalgia one has when opening a fortune cookie. To the unsaved hearer it sounds nice but holds no weight for them. Even though we understand and experience the power of His words, others have become or chosen to become spiritually deaf toward the inspired scripture. Thus, it becomes paramount that our actions speak louder than or just as loud as our words. If you encounter a person that is physically deaf, they use a form of communication called American Sign Language. Sign language is comprised of actions and gestures to express ideas or meaning. We need to learn a language to communicate with a spiritually deaf generation, communicating not solely with our words but also our actions to preach, teach, and show the love of Jesus. How do we do that? We must become servants and cultivate the same servant's heart that Jesus Himself exemplified.

1 John 3:18

"Dear children, let us not love with words or speech but with actions and in truth."

The most destructive persona in the body of Christ is someone who walks in the gifts of the Spirit yet refrains from living out the fruits of the Spirit. You can speak in tongues yet you cuss your neighbor out for his dog doing his business in your yard. You can cast out demons but raise hell and complain because the checkout line is too long at Walmart. Then finally, reaching the cashier with a horrible attitude, emitting darkness and dispelling light. You can preach fire from behind the pulpit, yet are demanding and rude to your server Sunday afternoon because she was slow to fill up your water. Then have the nerve to leave a tract or pamphlet about Jesus without leaving a tip, involuntarily or intentionally showing her that gesture that you care about your meal but don't care about her feeding the family she is working to support. I have personally spoke to many servers, and they will despondently tell me that they hate working Sundays. I assumed that it was because they were missing church. To my amazement, they said that because church folk were some of the most rude and demanding tables they had to serve. These should be moments they are looking forward to. Why? Because they should leave each table encouraged, prayed for, and financially blessed with a proper tip. These are just a few examples that happen every day in the body of Christ. Actions like this puts the paint brush in the hands of the unbeliever and inspires them to paint a picture of a rude, disrespectful, impatient, insensible, and callous Jesus.

There is no such thing as a perfect person. We all have our good days and bad days. Yet in spite of it all, we have to remember to be more like Jesus every day. The question to ponder is this. Through my actions and with sign languages, what message have I been communicating? What have I preached to my coworkers through my gestures?

What have I been showing my family and kids? *This world will not give the heart of God a chance if we keep misconstruing His character.* One the other side of the coin is when our actions and gestures are preaching Jesus during someone's time of need. When you visit someone in the hospital, that is showing him or her that you and the Jesus you live for cares. When you call someone who just lost a loved one you, with your actions, you are showing them that they aren't alone. When you aid in and give food to the homeless, you show them that they aren't forgotten. Thus, in return, you're painting a picture of Jesus in their hearts that reflects a faithful, loving, and caring Savior. We must have the fruit of the spirit growing or at least budding out of the gardens of our heart and given evidence through our actions.

Galatians 5:22–23

But the fruit of the Spirit is love, joy, peace, forbearance, kindness, goodness, faithfulness, [23] gentleness and self-control . . .

When we have a servant's heart, it puts the light we are meant to carry into action. Once again as the saying goes, "Actions speak louder than words." The kings of old in the book of 2 Chronicles were always intended to be the greatest servants; they were not intended to be the greatest dictators. When they were crowned and anointed as kings, they were also given a copy of the covenant, a written reminder of God and His words. If we are merely sitting on the throne and viewing everyone else as our loyal subjects, then we bake a cake of entitlement using ingredients of pride, ego, and selfishness. Yet once we understand that we have a mandate to serve our world, then society will become a better place. It will no longer be an emotional and spiritual "Black Friday" experience where we are stampeding over the back of others to catch a deal or sale. We must lift people up instead of pulling them down. Let's preach through sign language. We are the billboard of Jesus, the marketing plan of the heavenly realm. We are imperfect people, attempting to display the love of a perfect God. We must become true servants of Jesus to a nation and world that needs Jesus. A society, that was like that was in Bethesda, where the man at the stirred pool whom needed to jump in for healing, had encountered Jesus, yet we're screaming the same cry of the scriptural example in John Chapter 5 "I have no one to help me into the pool."

I Have No One

John 5:1–9

5 "After this there was a feast of the Jews, and Jesus went up to Jerusalem. 2 Now there is in Jerusalem by the Sheep Gate a pool, which is called in Hebrew, Bethesda, having five porches. 3 In these lay a great multitude of sick people, blind, lame, paralyzed, waiting for the moving of the water. 4 For an angel went down at a certain time into the pool and stirred up the water; then whoever stepped in first, after the stirring of the water, was made well of whatever disease he had. 5 Now a certain man was there who had an infirmity thirty-eight years. 6 When Jesus saw him lying there, and knew that he already had been in that condition a long time, He said to him, "Do you want to be made well?" 7 The sick man answered Him, "Sir, I have no man to put me into the pool when the water is stirred up; but while I am coming, another steps down before me." 8 Jesus said to him, "Rise, take up your bed and walk." 9 And immediately the man was made well, took up his bed, and walked." And that day was the Sabbath."

The man was lying on a mat for thirty-eight years, staring at the place of healing and longing to jump into the waters of restorations for more than three decades. Can you imagine the mental torture it must have seemed to feel as if you are so close yet so far away—gazing from the floor to witness a sick person rise out of the pool restored dripping a trail of water? Thirty-eight years he wished he could simply make his way into the pool after it was stirred. Have you ever felt like the invalid man? Feeling as if you are so close to your breakthrough, yet so far away, dwelling and swimming in depression contemplating the reasoning of being forgotten and possibly going through the database of your past experiences, thinking of all the other people you have helped when they needed it. Hitherto, you ask yourself, if they are such good friends, where are they now? Being in a state like this could allow the enemy to make your mind his zoo. The sentiment of rejection, abandonment, and relinquishment may have been the company that rang the doorbell, asking to come in to make itself at home. This was a place in life where despair no longer had to ask for direction because it visited your heart often. Yet, Jesus with a mission in mind to communicate using sign language, gestures of love, and the miraculous power He walked in, displayed actions of love and remembrance rather than rejection and loneliness. It is vital to notice in the scripture that the man didn't initiate the conversation with Jesus. He didn't attempt to grab the Son of God's attention because he was desperate. In fact, Jesus went to the man Himself. Could it be that he has simply coped with the issue, believing that this is how it is always going to be? Whatever the reason was, the apparent fact is Jesus searched out the nameless man who didn't asked to be found. Jesus is still looking to save, heal, and deliver in our day and time.

Hebrews 13:8 states, [8] Jesus Christ is the same yesterday and today and forever." Jesus precedes to ask the most insensitive and obvious question to the paralyzed man "Do you want to get well?" Like when doctors ask you to sign a consent form before they operate. Dr. Christ the great physician through scalpel of the anointing brings healing into this person's body. Yet, the response to Jesus's inquiry that the nameless man gave Jesus was unexpected. He tells Jesus that I have no one to take me to be pool—no help, no aide, and no assistance. He continues to describe the background of the drama taking place. "While I am trying to get in someone else goes down ahead of me." To be transparent, I scratched my head upon his response to Jesus and wondered why he was making excuses. This wasn't a moment to give the man a bunch of "if onlys." If only you would lived closer or if you would have called and reached out to someone for help. What if he did? What if he asked but no one answered? After all everyone else had their own issues. Why would they care about his? In that culture, some believed that sickness, infirmities, and disease was placed on someone because of a sin issue. Have you felt pushed away from a mistake you made? Perhaps you feel like the man laying by the pool and express the same words, a thought that you have no one to take you to the pool. Just remember in your darkest times and your times of despair God is there. *Keep in mind that just because you think that God is silent doesn't mean He is absent.* Jesus ultimately heals the man's body, and the man takes up his mat and walks away. Yet the overwhelming and constant thought that jumps out off the page is why didn't anyone take him to the pool? Where were the people who served him? Where were the people invested in his life and wanted to see him well? For thirty-eight years, he lay forgotten until Jesus walked by and remembered him. The message that Jesus was preaching to him via way of sign language was an act of love. Jesus served that man when no one else would. We as Christians are called to do the same. We must cultivate a heart of a servant in our day and time.

> Keep in mind that just because you think that God is silent doesn't mean He is absent.

Their Faith

Mark 2:1–12

"A few days later, when Jesus again entered Capernaum, the people heard that he had come home. ² They gathered in such large numbers that there was no room left, not even outside the door, and he preached the word to them. ³ Some men came, bringing to him a paralyzed man, carried by four of them. ⁴ Since they could not get him to Jesus because of the crowd, they made an opening in the roof above Jesus by digging through it and then lowered the mat the man was lying on. ⁵ When Jesus saw their faith, he said to the paralyzed man, "Son, your sins are forgiven." ⁶ Now some teachers of the law were sitting there, thinking to themselves, [7] "Why does this fellow talk like that? He's blaspheming! Who can forgive sins but God alone?"

[8] Immediately Jesus knew in his spirit that this was what they were thinking in their hearts, and he said to them, "Why are you thinking these things? [9] Which is easier: to say to this paralyzed man, 'Your sins are forgiven,' or to say, 'Get up, take your mat and walk'? [10] But I want you to know that the Son of Man has authority on earth to forgive sins." So he said to the man, [11] "I tell you, get up, take your mat and go home." [12] He got up, took his mat and walked out in full view of them all. This amazed everyone and they praised God, saying, "We have never seen anything like this!"

In this astounding passage of scripture, we read the story of six heroes. Jesus himself is eager to respond to the physical needs as well as address the judgment in the room toward the paralyzed man. The other champions in the story are the friends who valued the crippled man lying on the mat enough to do whatever was needed to get him to Jesus. Finally, recognition should also be given to the sick man who allowed them to carry him. As in an episode in one of my favorite childhood shows, *Reading Rainbow*, allow this passage to become alive and animated in your heart. Jesus, a man whose reputation preceded him, gathered a massive number of people, seeking an encounter with Him. Jesus the healer, deliverer, and Savior didn't solely minister with words but with demonstration. In a time before sci-fi movies and special effects, what they saw Jesus do blew their minds and was out of this world. Others gathered like the teachers of the law with an analytical attitude to find places to discredit and accuse Jesus. Like a music festival in a headliner band, the crowds were large. Yet in spite of the obstacles that had to be traversed, the paralyzed man had four friends who cared about him. They served a friend who couldn't serve himself. They didn't see breaking through the massive crowd as something that was impossible, rather just difficult. They had to think outside of the box and find a way to bring their friend to the healer. They exemplified true servanthood and were inundated with a love-fueled drive to reach their destination in the vicinity of Jesus because they were very aware of the résumé of the King of kings. Radical as it was, they got the idea to climb up the roof with the invalid man. Can you imagine the conversations that took place before they did the deed? Looking at each other, judging and weighing the cost. Thinking about how much it would cost to repair the damage gained from their pursuit. Whatever took place at that time, it didn't deter and discourage them from serving the need of their invalid friend. They hoisted him up to the roof and then started digging a hole. It was not a little hole where they can take a peek at Jesus or put their ear to the roof to listen, No, they dug an opening so large to lower a human body through. HGTV would have a fit (fit is southern talk for having a cow, and having a cow is southern talk for getting upset). Jesus is preaching the word to them in this crowded house, when all of sudden he hears a racket above him. Small pieces of the roof begin to fall on the ground. Little by little, the roof was being broken apart. It started as little snow flurries, and then it became a heavy snowstorm of dirt, sticks, and whatever materials were used to make the roof. Keep in mind the place was crowded and packed full of eager people hanging on the words of Jesus. The debris may have fallen on them.

> A hindrance is just an obstacle, not an impossibility.

Yet desperate times called for desperate measures, and they had to seize their moment with Jesus. A hindrance is just an obstacle, not an impossibility. Once the gap in the roof was large enough the faithful and servant-driven men lowered the afflicted man down from the roof in front of Jesus. Read the first words Jesus states when he sees the man and his friends closely. Mark 2:5 *"When Jesus saw their faith . . ."* Jesus acknowledged not only the faith of the man lying on the matt but also the ones that loved him enough to carry him. I believe this is a profound story that illustrates what having a servant heart looks like—not going to someone's house and randomly breaking down the roof like some confused Santa Claus, but truly helping the people around you. The difference from the invalid man at the pool of Bethesda and the paralyzed man lowered from the rooftop was that he had no one to serve him. Jesus was the consistent lifeline in both passages of scriptures, but friends with servant hearts played a vital role. Neither man could move himself. One man couldn't get to the pool after it was stirred, and the other man could never break through the crowd because he couldn't move.

Entitlement

We must learn how to serve those around us. We must serve our children with love and compassion yet with discipline. We must serve our spouse with sincerity and grace. We must serve our workplace with excellence and hard work. If we are going to be effective Christians, it is paramount to cultivate a servant's heart. The kings of 2 Chronicles's shortcoming occurred when they lost sight of the fact that the greatest leader must be the greatest servant. Maybe reading this, you came to the conclusion that you don't really have a servant's heart. If that is the fact, then start cultivating one. Ask yourself the question if you can celebrate others success before you own. Seek out the depths of your heart to discover the state of your humility. Start putting the attention and thoughts on someone else instead of your own needs all of the time. I once heard an amazing man of God, Pastor Jim Raley, author of *Hells Spells* and *Dream Killers*, say, "If you put your attention on the things that have God's attention, God will put His attention on the things that have yours." As the saying goes in the south "the world doesn't revolve around you." Have a servant's heart that is led by love rather than deceitful motives. Of course, there is balance; we must take care of ourselves and the needs we have. Even with this in mind, it is remarkable when we make the choice to help someone else, our needs are taken care of. We truly cannot outserve or outgive God as He directs us to do so. Everything that Jesus did in his life, death, and still today has been an act of love and a perfect display of servanthood. We must impersonate His character as Christians.

Ephesians 5:1

"Follow God's example, therefore, as dearly loved children"

The battle is waged within a person when entitlement and servant-hood face each other. They have been in conflict since the beginning of time and are still the tug of war within the heart of every person. Entitlement is often birthed in hurt and rejection. Therefore, you fight to keep what you think you deserve because of what you perceived to be withheld from you. The truth of this echoes far and wide from many circles and facets of life, from within families to nations and business offices to church establishments. The fight for control and having a voice is very real. There may be merit and reason from each side, but the conflict can be resolved or at least begin to find a resolution when entitlement leaves the room and servanthood has a seat. Entitlement only sees the success of the proprietor but not the big picture. Entitlement blinds the bearer to think that the only way for things to get done is if it is done their way. Don't get me wrong; when it is the 4th quarter of the game, the all-star needs to step up, but even then the star remembers that he or she isn't the only one on the team. They may be the best scorer, but without five people from your team stepping on the court to play the game of basketball, the game is forfeited. No matter what we may feel, the success we received is rarely achieved alone. Someone and somewhere along the way served your dream and vision. A teacher helped to educate you or a bus driver took you to school. Entitlement selfishly aids the bearer to believe that it is all about them. As a society, we would achieve much more if we spend more time serving each other and less time pulling each other down. I am six feet six inches tall and weigh more than three hundred pounds. I am a big boy and, yes, the struggle is very real trying to find clothes and buy shoes. Imagine if I were to approach a man with average strength and asked him to lift me up without aid or assistance from anyone else, requesting that he lift me completely up and place me feet first on a seat a few feet above the ground. It would be a hard undertaking, and some may deem it impossible. Yet if I was already standing on the chair, and without restricting him or holding on to anything, asked him to pull or push

> Entitlement is often birthed in hurt and rejection. Therefore, you fight to keep what you think you deserve because of what you perceived to be withheld from you.

me off the chair he could do it with ease. I know gravity fights against him and to overcome that, brute strength is required. However, to the average person it is easier for us to pull people down than it is for us to lift people up. Why? The physical and scientific answer to the question may be long and daunting, but from an emotional metaphor, the answer is simple. It's selfish-driven entitlement! We live in a culture that hungers for negativity and drama. As the quote from Norm Peterson says, "It's a dog eat dog eat world, Sammy, and I'm wearing Milkbone underwear." Sadly, it's this attitude of the heart that has stopped some churches and movements, its advancement.

The Battle between the Older and Younger Generations

The struggle between generations and cultures can be resolved with unity. The battle where younger and older generations of the faith use the name of each other as a pulley to yank down the reputation of someone to elevate the ego of their own must end. "Well I wouldn't do it this way" precedes comments of why they would do it better. It is a time in history when millennials may seem like a curse word and everything new is bad. Alternatively, if anyone has gray hair and doesn't wear skinny jeans or drink insanely difficult to pronounce and articulate the names of brands of coffee, then they are old, wrong, and outdated. If we are going to advance the movement of the cross, we must learn how to serve each other. If we are going to move the chain of revival across the fields of indifference for a first down to attempt a touchdown of awakening again and again, then we need to serve each other. The enemy is in hell, hanging out without a care in the world, because we, as the modern church, are too busy tearing each other up about the volume of the music being too loud, or whether the coffee can be drunk in the sanctuary, to give attention to the lost person that is hard of hearing walking into church for the first time with coffee in his hand. The distraction that is manufactured is from the horrible sweatshop of entitlement. Trying to multitask the Great Commission and an agenda led by entitlement simply doesn't work. As the Bible says, no one can serve two masters, and we need to make sure our pride isn't the slave driver with the whip of personal goals. By no means am I saying not to have aspirations, standards and ambitions; those are a must in life. Some people advance and others don't in different seasons of life. However, the name and legacy of the generation before you or behind you doesn't have to be the tread in the tires used to move up the road to your dreams. Bottom line, we are all better together. We are better when the experience of the seasoned saints is connected with the ingenuity of the millennials. Both contain giftings that shouldn't be ignored but celebrated.

Millennials

Please understand that just because something is old doesn't mean it is bad or wrong. The first word used to brand tradition is *religious*. In the mandate of not being religious, we will error in throwing away the baby with the bathwater. My heart is not to send you out in the backyard to grab your own switch for a whooping, as every southern child has done at some point in his or her life, but to share the importance of having a servant's heart. Understand as I write this book, I fall under the millennials age group. We can do so much for the kingdom, yet we carry a lot of demands with us. We at times can forget the process of serving because of a false belief that our degrees or our passions bypass that expectation. Maybe it is because we have been overlooked and overstepped that we have come to the conclusion that in order to be heard we must shout. Maybe the drive to be recognized has been due to the fact that many times, fathers and mothers of faith communicated commitment yet failed to follow through. Being overcommitted and underproductive is a recipe for broken relationships. Our generation has been struggling with an orphan spirit for so long. The pain can run even deeper when the one spiritually and earthly committed to mentor you failed to be consistent. Thus aids in birthing the person that beats their chest saying the words, "I'm just gonna do me." Meaning that I don't care about anyone else; I'm just going to look after me. If you have a disagreement with someone, go to the person and attempt to work it out. Don't make a Facebook status update about it or join a young pastor's Facebook page for a spirit-unled temper tantrum. Always remember submission isn't submission until there is a disagreement. Disagreement gives submission a chance to show up. So are you going to serve even though you don't agree? If you feel you can no longer serve the vision you are under, then move on. Unity doesn't simply mean agreement. Unity is coming alongside each other, noticing the differences but moving forward together because there is a common good. Let's not be so quick to leave the seasoned saints behind because we are scared to trust again. Let's not be so quick to throw away reverence because it is perceived as being old-fashioned.

> Always remember submission isn't submission until there is a disagreement. Disagreement gives submission a chance to show up.

The error with generations before us is to think that the anointed and respect is in the clothes and not the one wearing the clothes. God can move in boots and skinny jeans just as much as an Easter suit from K&G. We must cultivate a servant's heart. We have been branded as being lazy and not willing to work toward our goals. We have been labeled as wanting handouts yet with no sweat equality. We have learned to see obstacles that are difficult to achieve as being impossible to accomplish. We need to be Stephen in the book of Acts and serve the men and women of God who went before us. Be faithful to a place and be faithful to a vision. God will help you to navigate through what is healthy and what you need to cut away. God never intended the church to grow as one age group; we are all better together. We need the wisdom of the older generation, and they need vision of our day and time. If you want to get noticed and used, stay faithful, stay humble, and please stay consistent. Let God transition you; don't let frustration lead you to transition.

Older Generation

It is paramount that you learn how to differentiate between Christianity and church culture. The frustration that the younger generation is having with transitional churches is that they can't find a place for them to be themselves without their having to look like you. If you truly believe that a suit makes you more holy than jeans and a t-shirt, then you are in error. The excuse that has been used for decades is that we need to give God our Sunday best. First and foremost, that is nowhere in the Bible but are traditions that have been pass down from generation to generation. However, for the sake of context, let's say that God did require you to wear your Sunday best. For you, it may be the three-piece suit you got from Macys with Kenneth Cole gators, but for the twenty-five year old youth pastor, his Sunday best may not be a suit at all. To him it is the pair of concord 11s Jordan sneakers that he got for $220, a pair of Levi jeans, a swoop t-shirt and a fitted cap from the mall—not the suit he picked up from the thrift store to attend a wedding he was forced to go years ago. To him that is the presentation of his best to the Lord. His heart is in the right place, yet the tradition is what creates the conflict. Honor and submission is preached from the pulpit at the same time, slinging rocks labeled rebellion toward this generation. Thus, young people are leaving the church in masses or starting their own church or not going to church at all, using the excuse

> A church without any younger generations represented creates their own expiration date.

"I have nothing to wear." I have sat in the car heading to and from the airport with youth pastors, pouring out their hearts, desperately wanting to be fathered, yet they are rejected because they don't fit the physical mold of the tradition that has been deemed as sacred law. A church without any younger generations represented creates their own expiration date. Again, we must learn how to differentiate between Christianity and church culture. Having an usher who used to be bouncer with white gloves is a great tradition, but not having one isn't against the standards of the Bible. Not having a choir and just having a worship team isn't a sin; it's just not traditional. There is a massive cry and need for the millennial generation to be mothered and fathered. To address the orphan spirit attempting to figure out who they are and what they are called to do through trial and error. They are knocking on your office doors and sending you texts for coffee. They are the Joshua to your Moses and the Timothy to your Paul.

Don't be so busy that you forget about being effective. I am simply echoing the hearts of this generation that needs you to take action and care. Care beyond the numbers of attendees. Care beyond the color of the carpet and which "Wow 2000 Gospel Song" was played this past Sunday morning in the contemporary service. Care beyond the outfit that is worn or the style of hair. Simply care. They aren't lazy—well, most of them aren't. They are cause driven not just numbers driven. Now give them a cause that is worth chasing after. Cultivate a servant's heart and serve the younger generation.

We Are All Better Together.

Ephesians 4:3–6

"Make every effort to keep the unity of the Spirit through the bond of peace. [4] There is one body and one Spirit, just as you were called to one hope when you were called; [5] one Lord, one faith, one baptism; [6] one God and Father of all, who is over all and through all and in all."

Joshua and Moses had very similar tasks to overcome. Joshua being Moses's successor and Moses Joshua's mentor had approached a moment in their life when the task simply seemed impossible. After God sent Moses to deliver the Israelites from the bondage of slavery, he led them to freedom where they would soon be halted by a massive hindrance. Pharaoh was behind them with chariots and drawn weapons and the Red Sea was in front of them. God then instructed Moses to raise up his staff and when he did, the waters split and they were able to traverse across the Red Sea to safety. Similar but not identical Moses's mentee, Joshua had a comparable experience. Joshua was faced with the undertaking of crossing the Jordan River. Except this time God didn't instruct him to raise a staff. In fact, they had to get into the water and then witness the Jordan River split as like the Red Sea. Both Moses and Joshua witnessed the same results but had different methodologies. I firmly believe it is at the foundation of that point where most of the conflict between generations are waged. "That is not how we used to do it" and "Why won't we try it this way"? Let's stop being so entangled with methodologies that we can't celebrate the miracles that God is trying to do in our midst. We are all better together. The multimedia and social media knowledge a young person brings to the table is impressive. The years of experiences and wisdom from the word of God and leadership of the older generation is needed. When we start being more like Jesus and cultivate a servant's heart, we will finally advance the kingdom of God instead of slinging stones from the personal kingdoms we have created.

Matthias and Stephen

Acts 1:21–26

"Therefore it is necessary to choose one of the men who have been with us the whole time the Lord Jesus was living among us, [22] beginning from John's baptism to the time when Jesus was taken up from us. For one of these must become a witness with us of his resurrection."

[23] So they nominated two men: Joseph called Barsabbas (also known as Justus) and Matthias. [24] Then they prayed, "Lord, you know everyone's heart. Show us which of these two you have chosen [25] to take over this apostolic ministry, which Judas left to go where he belongs." [26] Then they cast lots, and the lot fell to Matthias; so he was added to the eleven apostles."

There was place for advancement due to Judas self-inflicted demise. A couple prerequisites were set in place to find the one who would step up into the apostolic ministry. First, they had been with them during the time span Jesus was alive. Secondly, they had to witness Jesus resurrection. They were looking for someone near their life experiences. Maybe Matthias was near their age but even if he wasn't he shared in their memories. They prayed and cast lots, which is like drawing straws, and then Matthias was voted in as part of the apostles from the Bible based board. What should this tell us? That Matthias was faithful to serve all the years of Jesus life. He was present during His ministry and his resurrection. Before a title and before a position he was there. Matthias was faithfully rooted and God advanced him because of it. Stay faithful to your call. Stay faithful to your mission. Cultivate a servant's heart, serve your community, and make Jesus famous. Maybe you didn't have the opportunity to grow up with the seasoned people around the table. Yet you know there is a calling on your life to advance the mission of Jesus. If you don't represent the old generation that shared life experiences like Matthias, but simply have a drive in your heart to make Jesus's name great. If that is you then the assignment is simple. Keep serving!

Acts 6:2–7

"So the Twelve gathered all the disciples together and said, "It would not be right for us to neglect the ministry of the word of God in order to wait on tables. ³ Brothers and sisters, choose seven men from among you who are known to be full of the Spirit and wisdom. We will turn this responsibility over to them ⁴ and will give our attention to prayer and the ministry of the word."

⁵ This proposal pleased the whole group. They chose Stephen, a man full of faith and of the Holy Spirit; also Philip, Procorus, Nicanor, Timon, Parmenas, and Nicolas from Antioch, a convert to Judaism. ⁶ They presented these men to the apostles, who prayed and laid their hands on them.

⁷ So the word of God spread. The number of disciples in Jerusalem increased rapidly, and a large number of priests became obedient to the faith."

Stephen was chosen to take up the call of ministry while he was serving. He waited tables and cleaned up messes as he was doing ministry. What an amazing example of cultivating a servant's heart. Serving the tables of the Generals of faith that went before you so they can advance the message of the good news. Stephen, full of the Holy Spirit, would end up dying for the sake of the gospel. He gave his life preaching truth. Nevertheless, what is so important to see was that he was not just called to preach he was called to serve. We must get back to the heart of a servant because this is the foundation of our ministries. Do you love the Lord enough to wash tables after a banquet? Do you love the Lord enough to help your wife clean up the playroom? Do you love your ministry enough to set up tables and vacuum floors? We should never grab the mic to preach if we aren't willing to grab a broom. I remember watching the pastors in my life mimic what true ministry looks like. I watched Pastor Michael Kim Snyder from First Assembly of God in Asheboro, NC install toilet seats in the church. I remember him opening the door for his wife Pastor Connie and her bragging about how he makes her coffee with whip cream every morning. He served his church and his family. I remember watching my Pastors Ron and Joy Hawkins take time out of there insanely busy schedules to go paintballing with a bunch of teenagers and young adults. I watched them as they aided in the community care outreach in Fort Wayne, Indiana, yet also deeply served the needs of the young and older people alike in his church. I witnessed firsthand, my pastor, Jamie Jones the author of a life changing book called " The Left Handed Warrior" and lead pastor of Trinity Church in Deltona, Florida, install lights in the sanctuary or spend hours painting the walls for the churches massive remodel. I watched as Pastor Michelle the wife of Pastor Jamie serve the needs of the entire church even as she was walking through her fight with breast cancer in which she overcame. I watched her start an amazing ministry called "Brave is beautiful" which sends out faith filled care packages for people walking though cancer. What am I saying? I saw all of them, many times, in ministry lead by example. They led by serving and that is how we need to do it. They never asked anyone to do something that they haven't already done or weren't willing to do themselves. Crowns are greater than trophies and we need to cultivate a servant's heart, and always keep that in mind.

CHAPTER 11
CROWNED WITH VICTORY

We are under attack. A great war has been waged against us and our families. This battle hasn't just started, but has been fought from generations to generations. There is an epic and enormous battle with legions of enemies encamped on the battlefield waiting to lay siege. The onslaught is consistent and lingering. It may have appeared that the enemy has won and laid waste to all hope because many times the opponent simply quit fighting. The enemy is equipped with an extreme weapon and uses it to disarm the would-be warriors. The weapon of mass destruction is fear. Fear will persuade the warrior to lay down their arms because the battle may seem impossible to win. Fear is the arrow the enemy attempts to launch in the mind of every believer. This may sound like an epic battle in history yet; it's the daily transaction in all of our lives. There is a war being fought over you and in you, whether you show up to fight or not. Fear of the unknown, fear of failure or even fear of trying all aids in the continuation of choices trampling over the peace and well-being of our lives. The battle that is taking place even as you are reading this book is happening right now; a combat for your soul and spirit. It's time that we pull out the blood covered arrow shot in our hearts and come to the conclusion that we will not be bullied. Fear does one of two things. Fear will keep you silent and startled like a deer caught in headlights. Or fear will cause you to run like a cat being chased by a dog. Don't become so overwhelmed by the circumstances around you and in your family that fear silences you. Don't allow fear to force you to be frozen in worry and anxiety. Fight off the desire to run away from the issues and tribulations. Instead of being silent and running away from the challenges within, make a stand and hold your ground.

THE LOADOUT

Ephesians 6:10–18

"Finally, be strong in the Lord and in his mighty power. [11] Put on the full armor of God, so that you can take your stand against the devil's schemes. [12] For our struggle is not against flesh and blood, but against the rulers, against the authorities, against the powers of this dark world and against the spiritual forces of evil in the heavenly realms. [13] Therefore put on the full armor of God, so that when the day of evil comes, you may be able to stand your ground, and after you have done everything, to stand. [14] Stand firm then, with the belt of truth buckled around your waist, with the breastplate of righteousness in place, [15] and with your feet fitted with the readiness that comes from the gospel of peace. [16] In addition to all this, take up the shield of faith, with which you can extinguish all the flaming arrows of the evil one. [17] Take the helmet of salvation and the sword of the Spirit, which is the word of God. [18] And pray in the Spirit on all occasions with all kinds of prayers and requests. With this in mind, be alert and always keep on praying for all the Lord's people.

Even with every day occurrences, we dress for the occasion. If you work in construction, you don't wear a three-piece suit but work boots and jeans. If you are a doctor, you aren't laying out shoulder pads, cleats and a helmet the night before. We prepare ourselves physically for the assignments that we have entrusted our lives to steward. In the same way, no solider saunters into war with a tee shirt and flip-flops armed with a can do attitude and sunblock. That person will quickly become a casualty because they weren't dressed or prepared for the battle at hand. Knowing that you are going to walk into war you will gather the proper *Loadout*. Maybe your primary weapon is an SBR (short-barreled Rifle) AR15 rifle with a Trijicon Acog companied with plenty of filled 30 round Magpul magazines. You will take a full-size handgun as your secondary, like a tried and true Glock 17, with extra 17 round magazines, and maybe a few 33 rounds stored away. It would still be in error to have the tools to fight in the war but not to protect your body. Warriors would grab their plate carrier with all sorts of well thought out amenities attached to it. Not items that look "tactical-cool" but literally aid in being tactical. On the vest would be a place to carry the magazines as well as a med kit that would include quick clot and a tourniquet, maybe a radio or a way to communicate with fellow brothers in arms. The prepared soldier would have a helmet to protect him or herself with attachments needed for the mission or simply the survival of the fight. Lastly, they won't go into battle wearing bowling shoes or crocs but boots that will aid in traversing the grounds and making a stand. Yet with all the tools and gear, the battle would be lost quickly if the solider didn't know how to wield them under pressure. Yes, at a gun range standing still getting a few inch groupings may seem like a big deal, or at home running dry fire drills with tactical reloads works for a cool social media video. Nevertheless, in the heat of battle when all the fine motor skills may leave for a moment and adrenaline rushes in, it doesn't become a desire to just look the part but demands the answer are you ready for the fight? A famous quote that some accredits to Archilochus and used in the military and other tactical training is "*We don't rise to the level of our expectations; we fall to the level of our training.*" *You* can spend $2000 on an amazing Daniel defense AR15 but if you didn't train to remove the thumb safety you will die in the heat of battle.

Even Paul as he wrote Ephesians to the church of Ephesus was sharing with them about the fight before he ever spoke about the tools in detail. In Chapter 6 verse 10 Paul addresses where the empowerment to win the fight comes from. Like in the 90's Power Rangers show, taking out the "morphers" yelling "its morphing time" to transform and put on a suit equipping them to perform at a higher, mighty, and powerful level. Likewise, when we are in Jesus and put on Jesus we become "strong in the Lord and in His mighty power." Next Paul commands the reader to put on the full and complete armor of God. Don't walk into battle with your boots but forget your breastplate. Paul made it clear to put on the full armor of God. As we mentioned in a previous chapter we are taking a stand again the devils schemes, not simply his demonic lies but also his planes, methods, and procedures. God has a plan for our life and the enemy is on a mission to impede it. This plan is implemented through choices that are celebrated and welcomed, behaviors that are counseled to be celebrated when God doesn't tolerate it. It does often present itself as drug abuse and being strung out in an alley throwing away family and life itself. Many people don't wake up to aspire to be a crack head but often that road began by unhealthy relationship choices. It is important that we give adequate attention to Paul next words because it lays out very clearly and directly who or what we are fighting. The error is to think that you are just fighting family members and people in general. Yet that is only the avenue and vehicle the enemy uses to drive through and over people's lives. Paul directs the attention to the spiritual battle there; the struggle is not against flesh and blood. The fight is against the authorities and against the powers of this dark world. It isn't simply a person or a boss; it is the strongman that needs to be bound in our lives and over our families. You are declaring war. Not over your father, sister, sibling or other families members. No! You are declaring war against the demonic influences that has made itself at home and ripped through generations for far too long. You are battling the spirit behind the depression not the one who is depressed. You are fighting the spirit behind the panic attacks not the person having the panic attacks. The fight is real and it is only growing. It is not going to be resolved with a hollow point to the spiritual enemy. There is a spiritual problem, but also a spiritual, yet practical remedy.

2 Corinthians 10:4–5

"The weapons we fight with are not the weapons of the world. On the contrary, they have divine power to demolish strongholds. [5] We demolish arguments and every pretension that sets itself up against the knowledge of God, and we take captive every thought to make it obedient to Christ."

Thus, Paul brings the fight into proper prospective. It demands the thought to no longer just ask "who" the problem is but ask "Why" the problem exists in the first place. He brings everything back into focus in verse 13 with a conjunction verb "Therefore." "Therefore, put on the full armor of God so what when the day of evil come, you may be able to stand your ground, and after you done everything to stand. Stand firm . . ." The Bible doesn't say if the day of evil comes but when it comes. It's not a question of if we will walk through the heat of battle or not, it's simply a matter of when. We will all go thought hardships, but when the dust settles will you and your dreams be lying cold on the battlefield, or standing firm, beaten and bruised, but alive? The comforting outlook in all of this is the simple yet profound fact that we won't have to fight alone. Jesus is fighting with us and empowered us to win. Paul mentioned standing more times that he did fighting. Why? Because standing firm and not being moved is a fight in itself. As you make the effort to break generational curses off your life by practical choices people may make fun of you. They may ridicule you for not engaging in the same unhealthy activities you used to. Your own family members may attempt to weaponize your relationship with Jesus by saying that you are "holier than thou." Nevertheless, don't give attention to that and remember what you are fighting. Don't lose your ground, convictions, and standards through intimidation via the same tactics the enemy uses. Friends, family, and coworkers may gossip about you because you want to wait to have sex until you are married. Remember the fight isn't a "who" but a "what." Those engaging in gossip are French kissing the devil himself, entangling their tongue with his while receiving his DNA thorough vocal and oral exchange.

> Those engaging in gossip are French kissing the devil himself, entangling their tongue with his while receiving his DNA thorough vocal and oral exchange. Conveying the same rooted message from the pits of hell which is to rob, kill and destroy.

Conveying the same rooted message from the pits of hell which is to rob, kill and destroy. Hold your ground. Dig your heels in the dirt and keep standing. Remember why you are fighting as you withstand the times that the "day of evil comes." Your children are worth standing for. Your peace is worth standing for. Your future is worth standing for. Your legacy is worth standing for. You are worth standing for.

Belt of Truth

Wear the belt of truth at all times. The imagery behind the armor of God wasn't a medieval knight but a roman solider. The belt was of importance because the sword, and other articles, was attached to it. Paul starts off telling us to wear this belt because it is the most important aspect of the armor of God; it is truth that holds everything together. Truth that keeps us standing against all the flaming arrows of lies shot in our direction. If we don't believe the fight is worth fighting then why keep standing. The devil can't make you do anything but he can persuade us to do it. He can take the ground we gave up. He did it in the garden with Adam and Eve with one question "Did God really say." They gave up their ground and authority. The deceiver attempted to do it against Jesus after his time of fasting when he came to tempt Him. However, Jesus knowing truth and being truth in flesh withstood the lies of the enemy. Keeping standing and put on the belt of truth, be firmly aware that the Truth Himself is standing with you.

John 14:6

"Jesus answered, "I am the way and the truth and the life. No one comes to the Father except through me."

Breastplate of Righteousness

Protect your heart and your vital organs. One right placed shot and the fight is all over. If the enemy can shoot his poisoned dart into your heart then everything else will be effected. The fight won't seem worth it and the effort will seem pointless. One of the roman soldier's breastplate called "Lorica segmentata" was made out of individual segmented iron plates woven together with leather. It would be layered one top of each other and was found to be a superior breastplate to chain mail. What is significant about this is that the soldier had to have help with putting on his armor. They needed help to tighten up the armor so that it was snug and could be used appropriately as protection. This brings an important truth that we need accountability in our lives as we fight the fight of faith. Someone who can come to you and if they see an area slipping can lovingly help you tighten the behavior up. You need a trusted person involved in your fight that can aid you in abstaining from smoking anymore because they know you are trying to quite. You need an encourager present to tighten up your armor and bring correction if need be.

Proverbs 12:1

"Whoever loves discipline loves knowledge, but whoever hates correction is stupid"

Feet Fitted with the Gospel of Peace

This is vital because in war life is going to push against you. The Roman soldier's shoes weren't a large metal boot, rather a sandal looking cleat that was appropriate for their tactic of battle. At the bottom of the shoes were tiny balls of metal that would give traction. This needed stability was vital. They need to be stable yet swift. The shoes are always the foundation of a battle tactic called "Testudo" which involved the interlocking of shields. We need to wear feet fitted with the gospel of Peace so we will not be moved in the storms of battle. It is very possible to have peace in the mist of total conflict. This is not acting like the problem doesn't exist, but knowing that God has it all under control. The deep understanding that Jesus is walking with us in our valley and that we can take courage in the hardest of times. Every step and every stable position, He is there with us.

Joshua 1:9

"Have I not commanded you? Be strong and coura-
geous. Do not be afraid; do not be discouraged, for
the Lord your God will be with you wherever you go."

Shield of Faith

The shield that the romans carried was a heavy and large tool. It wasn't
only used to protect themselves from spears, arrows, a strike of the
sword and other forms of battery from the enemy, but was also used as
a weapon in itself. For ultimate protection against a rain of arrows, a
unit of soldiers would perform a tactic called the "Testudo or tortoise
formation." They would take their shields and interlock them so there
was protection from all areas. "Plutarch describes this formation as
used by Mark Antony during his invasion of Parthia in 36 BC: Then
the shield-bearers wheeled round and enclosed the light-armed troops
within their ranks, dropped down to one knee, and held their shields
out as a defensive barrier. The men behind them held their shields
over the heads of the first rank, while the third rank did the same for
the second rank. The resulting shape, which is a remarkable sight,
looks much like a roof, and is the surest protection against arrows,
which just glance off it."" [i] In order to have this level of protection
someone had to take a knee. What an amazing point that illustrates
the power of prayer that feeds our faith in times of battle. When we
lift up the shield of faith it smoothers out the fiery arrows the enemy
attempts to launch in our directions. I firmly believe that the faith
that we are lifting up during the times of battle isn't faith in our faith,
but the shield that is being exalted is the faith in God's faithfulness.
In the heat of the moment, when standing firm becomes more difficult remember how Jesus has been faithful. When David returned to
camp Ziklag after marching with his men in 1 Samuel 30, everything
that he and his men owned and loved was taken and carried off. The
camp was burnt down and nothing was left. In the moment of great
tragedy, people were blaming David and talked about stoning him.
Nevertheless, David elevated his shield of faith in that moment.

1 Samuel 30:6 King James Version (KJV)

". . . but David encouraged himself in the Lord his God."

What did David dwell upon in that moment that he would find encouragement? This was before David prayed and talked with God; this was an internal conversation that took place in crisis. I believe that David remembered everything God had done for him and how faithful He is. Right after David encouraged himself, he asked for the Ephod, spoke with God, and received direction to take everything the enemy had stolen back. We must remember that we serve a faithful God. When you want to quit the fight, remember the testimonies of victory that you have already experienced.

Psalm 91:3–5

[3] Surely, he will save you from the fowler's snare and from the deadly pestilence.
    [4] He will cover you with his feathers, and under his wings you will find refuge; his faithfulness will be your shield and rampart. [5] You will not fear the terror of night, nor the arrow that flies by day,"

Helmet of Salvation

Take up arms today and remember why you are fighting. Arm and equip yourself with the armor of God. These are articles meant to be worn to make war and win the fight of faith. Put on the helmet of salvation, which protects your thought life. A roman soldier's helmet had openings around the ears, and the face was uncovered. This was important so they can see the battlefield without anything blocking there vision. In addition, they must be able to hear the commands of the leader who is giving orders on how to fight. A strong aspect of roman warfare is that they fought in units with great skills. However, in order to follow the order you must hear the orders. Put on the helmet of salvation and protect your thought life. Open your ears to hear the commands of the general of our faith, Jesus Christ, directing your path. Protect your thought life and use Gods words as the filter that sifts through all the lies.

Ephesians 4:22–24

"You were taught, with regard to your former way of life, to put off your old self, which is being corrupted by its deceitful desires; [23] to be made new in the attitude of your minds; [24] and to put on the new self, created to be like God in true righteousness and holiness."

The Sword of the Spirit

A sword that the roman solders carried was called the Gladius. It was a double edge sword that was highly effective in combat. The sword and shield were used together in conflict. Lined up for battle the army would advance upon hearing the vocal commands, the brothers in arms carrying the shield would push against the enemy, and the moment the opportunity presented itself the other soldiers would stab using their sword. This was a brutal yet highly effective tactic. Likewise, the shield of faith and the sword of the spirit can never be separated. The Word of God is the sword that we wield every day. Forged with metals of God's faithfulness and His infallible words we can combat the lies and pressures the enemy hurls toward us. Far too long the body of Christ has acted like feeble defenseless believers and allowed the enemy to nest in our homes. Enough is enough, swing the word of God, and sever the head of the strongman of addiction, suicide, depression, sexual sin, or whatever has slithered its way up your family tree. Jesus fought the enemy with the word. When we know the Word of God, we know truth. Moreover, if we know truth, we have a standard to decipher the lies.

Hebrews 4:12

"For the word of God is alive and active. Sharper than any double-edged sword, it penetrates even to dividing soul and spirit, joints and marrow; it judges the thoughts and attitudes of the heart."

Pray in the Spirit

Lastly, Paul tells us in Ephesians 6 to "pray in the spirit on all occasions . . ." When we pray we are always connected to our lifeline. When we pray we are being coached and encouraged by God himself. When we pray we are being strengthened to continue the fight of standing. Not retreating, not holding back, or quitting the fight. Prayer is our war cry that prepares and aids in the conflict of fighting this spiritual battle. When the romans were lined up for battle staring the enemy in the eye, they would take their sword and slam in against their shields. Along with that intense and unified rhythm, they would give an intense war cry and shout. When we are standing firm and doing all else to stand we must connect our shield of faith, His word which is the Sword of the Spirit and our prayer life. When all three of these vital truths are in place, we will find victory on the other end of the battlefield. Put on the armor of God daily and make siege against the generational bondage in your life and your family's lives. Your consistent actions will bring constant victory. Hold your ground, don't retreat, and keep standing.

Hebrews 10:39

"But we do not belong to those who shrink back and are destroyed, but to those who have faith and are saved."

Crowned with Victory

If something is going to change it isn't going to happen because of wishful thinking but with effort and giving it thoughtful attention. On the other end of the battlefield, you will be crowned with victory as chains are broken and lifestyles are changed. The reward would be noticed when your children grow up in a healthy marriage with mom and dad present and actively involved. The Crown of victory is earned when poverty is broken off your back and you no longer have to worry how you are going to feed your family. Trophies were given because of what was achieved, but crowns were earned because of what was fought to obtain. Romans would receive crowns as a symbol of their great exploits obtained in combat. None, of the crowns, was given because of something that only benefited the receiver, but it was an act of bravery that aided Romans and their fellow brother in arms. It wasn't a simple tarnishing trophy but an earned crown. The "Civic Crown" was given because a roman citizen saved the lives of another roman citizen. They had to fight and kill the enemy that day. It was an act of bravery that saved lives. The "Grass Crown" was earned by a roman solider that saved an entire legion or army of roman soldiers. The very grass used to create the crown was taken from the battlefield in which they completed the heroic feat. There are many other crowns given to those who put there life on the line for others. They were crowned with victory. As you are making a stand and drawing a line in the sand, know that you are fighting for victory. Think about how years later someone is going to call you to say thank you for stopping the pattern. Thank you for going to college, thank you for stopping the drinking. Thank you for finding professional help and medical attention. Who is going to thank you and crown you with victory because you refused to quit. Remember whom you are fighting for even though it seems that others are fighting against you. Our great example, Jesus Christ, fought for all mankind with love and prevailing passion even while others were fighting against him. The Roman soldiers' flogged Him, beat Him, and ridiculed Him. Moreover, in their own sarcastic way, they forced a crown of thorns on His head that pierced his head. They thought

> Trophies were given because of what was achieved, but crowns were earned because of what was fought to obtain.

they were mocking him but they were crowning Him with victory! Pilate had a sign made that was placed on the cross for all to see with the words "Jesus of Nazareth, the King of the Jews." They thought they were mocking Him but were only highlighting His prophetic mission. He is not only the King of Kings but He is also the Lord of Lords. Our savior was crowned with victory. He didn't quit. He didn't stop. He kept fighting and when it was time He fought by dying. Yet three days later rose from the dead physically representing and echoing the truth that He always walked in, which is victory. Jesus never lost sight of why he was fighting. He was fighting for you and me.

John 10:18

"No one takes it from me, but I lay it down of my own accord. I have authority to lay it down and authority to take it up again. This command I received from my Father."

CHAPTER 12
RESTORING THE ALTAR OF THE DINNER TABLE

One of my favorite television shows to watch is a show hosted by Andrew Zimmerman. It is a show called "Bizarre Foods." I am that person that some may call a "Foodie." Mr. Zimmerman travels all around the world and eats food that may seem bizarre to us but is common to those of that culture. From exotic fish, to guinea pigs he eats it all. Above all the food, what I truly enjoy about the show is how he sits at the dinner table and fellowships with the people. Breaking cultural division, religious boundaries, social and economic divides. Sitting at the table in hostile countries laughing and hugging each other to indigenous tribes around the world smiling, which breaks the language barrier at the dinner table. I am amazed watching this show because they are finding community and love at the dinner table.

My heart in writing this book is that both individuals and families would start to talk about the issues going on in their lives, problems that have been ignored, while we act as if they don't exist. Problems that cause someone to blow up and storm out the house every time they are brought up thus are never talked about. My heart is that the person hurting in silence would find the strength to speak up. I prayed repeatedly over this book that as you read the words people and situations would come to mind that you would know demands your attention. I desire for families to start talking about their issues or problems. At the dinner table, I desire that fathers would take their rightful place as the priest of the home and create a sanctuary where love, peace, and joy reside; that at the altar of the dinner table situations and problems are laid down in conversation so the bearer won't have to carry it alone. In the atmosphere during dinner, there will be times of casting vision and encouragement. Parents letting their children know that they aren't alone. My prayer has been that the dinner table would be the altar that problems are placed at and Jesus' love consumes. At the altar of the dinner table, lives will be altered. In time, teenagers will know that they can let their parents into the private pains of their lives because they are cared about and heard. Life keeps us busy and schedules can get crazy. Nevertheless, if families would designate a time to gather around the altar of the dinner table at least once a week I truly believe breakthrough would occur. I am not saying build some weird altar to eat your dinner on but to create space in fellowship, community, and conversation in your family.

How different would Kings Joash, Amaziah, and Uzziah lives have been if they gave attention to reoccurring behavior. What would their legacy look like if they communicated about the covenant that they promised to keep around the dinner table? In our fast pace life where time is money we need to invest that time in the stock of our families. When you die, the new car won't be at your deathbed, but hopefully if you live your life correctly the family that you invested in will be. Crowns are greater than trophies. Finding time to have a life shared with the ones we love and are working to provide for, is a constant tug of war. I understand the predicament as we all face it. However, we must draw the conclusion that quality time is needed, and honesty and transparency are welcomed at the altar of the dinner table. A time that pride is swallowed and humility is the main course. Making time in spite of the extracurricular activities to worship Jesus and talk to each other at the altar of the dinner table.

Pray for them not about them

Sitting at the altar of the dinner table is a perfect time to laugh, have fun and talk about the day, but it is also the

Pray for them not about them.

perfect time to pray for the needs of everyone around the table. Let your family know that you are there to serve each other. We spend so much of our time serving everyone else that sometimes our family gets the leftovers. Pray for them, as they are transparent about what is going on. *Pray for them not about them.* Praying about someone is like undercover gossip and slander. However, praying for them is intercession that gains God's attention. Pray for the strength to resist the temptation the young man is fighting while in school or the insecurities the sixteen-year-old teenage daughter is battling within herself. If you address it while it is a seed, it won't have to be radically cut down after it's grown into a tree. Give attention to the insecurity before it grows up to depression and she is cutting her thighs. Talk about the situation of fighting the temptation of lust before it grows up to a pornographic addiction. Steward the garden of your family at the altar of the dinner table. Here are four practical steps that can aid in starting the talk in your home and break the pattern of behavior that has identified itself within your family; the tapeworm that had been the parasite consuming the life in your home.

Talk to each other

Talk to each other! This in and of itself seems like an elementary and simple place to start. Yet to sit around the dinner table and eat while everyone is on his or her cell phone removes an opportunity to talk. If we are not careful we can become more invested in our digital communities than we are in our physical communities. Put the phones down for a moment and talk. In order to effectively talk, you must be willing to listen. Hear each other out; that old saying "children should only been seen and not heard" is horrible and will create complete dysfunction. The personal struggle of the little girl worried about their lost cat is important to her so it should be important to mom and dad. Often times before we give credit to the magnitude of a situation we weigh it against how bad our own battles are. Yes, the lost cat may not be as vital as paying the mortgage on time but it is important nonetheless. If we fail, in moments like this, to listen when it is seemingly childish, why would they speak to us when they want to try drugs and it is serious? Teenagers, these are the great moments that if you will listen you can learn a lot about your parents. Why they are the way, they are. Learn from there life experiences and mistakes. You may be amazed by the wisdom they have because they have been in your shoes before. *Know it all's will never learn anything at all!*

Pray for each other

When the need is known, help each other and take it to Jesus. The devil hates it when a family prays for each other. He wants them to slander, gossip, and complain not pray. However, when you find your inner "Rocky" and wage war in the spirit hell will take notice. Talking about our problems and laying them at the feet of Jesus is what He desires. Around the altar of the dinner table where one by one people are sharing their prayer request, it is giving parents accurate, truthful information such that they know how to subdue and guard the land. Resourcing them with the information to invite Jesus in the problem thus, He himself becomes the solution. When we allow Jesus to come into our problems, He will direct and counsel us to victory.

Celebrate for each other

Around the altar of the dinner table is the chance to celebrate each other. Celebrate the victories as well as the progress. Parents, give genuine information regarding how you noticed the effort your kids are making. Maybe they washed the dishes without being told or aced a test at school. Take and find moments to celebrate each other. Kids, maybe you noticed your parents choose to stop smoking and they have officially gone one week without a cigarette, take that moment to commend them. Families should walk with each other during the darkest valleys and on the brightest mountaintops.

These are all simple directions but applying them to your lives will make an epic difference. Don't just tell each other that you care show them that you care. Even if the circumstances may seem impossible, it is amazing how quickly things can turn around when Jesus is invited to work. Crowns are greater than trophies. Yes, the food on the table was paid for with effort and time but the fellowship around the table is proof and the reason why the effort was needed.

Raise the Banner

Exodus 17:8–15

"The Amalekites came and attacked the Israelites at Rephidim. ⁹ Moses said to Joshua, "Choose some of our men and go out to fight the Amalekites. Tomorrow I will stand on top of the hill with the staff of God in my hands." ¹⁰ So Joshua fought the Amalekites as Moses had ordered, and Moses, Aaron and Hur went to the top of the hill. ¹¹ As long as Moses held up his hands, the Israelites were winning, but whenever he lowered his hands, the Amalekites were winning. ¹² When Moses' hands grew tired, they took a stone and put it under him and he sat on it. Aaron and Hur held his hands up—one on one side, one on the other—so that his hands remained steady till sunset. ¹³ So Joshua overcame the Amalekite army with the sword.
¹⁴ Then the Lord said to Moses, "Write this on a scroll as something to be remembered and make sure that Joshua hears it, because I will completely blot out the name of Amalek from under heaven." ¹⁵ Moses built an altar and called it The Lord is my Banner."

The assignment was simple just keep your hands lifted and you will win. However, just like anyone his arms got tired. He would have failed his task if he didn't have two people who were aware of his mission and cared about not only Moses's wellbeing, but also of Joshua's and the Israelites. They sat him on a rock and one on each side served Moses by holding up his arms when he couldn't do it by himself thus aiding Joshua to victory. This is a powerful passage of scripture that highlights the importance of not fighting alone. He had people who cultivated a servant's heart in a hard time in his life. If we will make our times with our families important, we will then have the information about their battle and the opportunity to hold up their arms thus finding victory. Even thinking about Moses, Aaron, and Hur creates the mental picture of victory. Moses seated on the rock and his two friends extending his arms above his head positioned like a "V." If we, as a society would serve each other and talk about problems without it turning into arguments and inward fighting we will see the change we desire. When it was all over, Moses built an altar and called it "Jehovah Nissi" which means the lord is my banner.

"Nes" is sometimes translated as a flag with an emblem or crest attached to it. In battle, opposing nations would fly their own flag on a pole at each of their front lines. This was to give their soldiers a feeling of hope and a focal point when they looked at them. It was a focal point that encouraged them when they looked at it and was a reminder to them why they were fighting and whom they were fighting for. God is our banner that we wave and is encouragement to give us hope and a focal point. Make it a mission as you restore the altar of the dinner table to wave the banner of Jesus as a reminder of who you are fighting for and who is fighting for you. In one of the hardest moments in my life, Psalm 121 became the banner that I waved in my heart.

Psalm 121

> ¹ I lift up my eyes to the mountains—
> where does my help come from?
> ² My help comes from the Lord,
> the Maker of heaven and earth.
> ³ He will not let your foot slip—
> he who watches over you will not slumber;
> ⁴ indeed, he who watches over Israel
> will neither slumber nor sleep.
> ⁵ The Lord watches over you—
> the Lord is your shade at your right hand;

⁶ the sun will not harm you by day, nor the moon
by night.
⁷ The Lord will keep you from all harm— he will
watch over your life;
⁸ the Lord will watch over your coming and going
both now and forevermore."

This verse gave me strength and encouragement to keep going even though I didn't feel like it. It reminded me to keep fighting and gave attention to the why I am fighting. It helps to constantly redirect my focal point to think about the victory rather than the daily stress of the battle.

Philippians 4:8

⁸ "Finally, brothers and sisters, whatever is true, whatever is noble, whatever is right, whatever is pure, whatever is lovely, whatever is admirable—if anything is
excellent or praiseworthy—think about such things."

I pray that you will start to restore the altar of your dinner table and invite Jehovah Nissi "the LORD is our banner" at the seat of honor. Allow Him to make siege in the kingdom of your home, knocking down conceded trophies. Thus, once he has conquered your heart lay your crown at His feet submitting under his reign. You will be much better off. Why? Because Crowns are Greater than Trophies.

ABOUT THE AUTHOR

Timothy McCain is a much sought after international evangelist and founder of Opening Eyes Ministries. He has a heart for the lost and for stirring the embers of revival. He, his wife Madai and son Hezekiah travel to the nations and share a message of hope birthed from their own personal experience of pain and adversity.

With a unique approach of transparency, and no-nonsense messaging they have seen thousands make commitments to the Lord. Timothy's desire is for people to have a true encounter with the Lord that supersedes any mere religious experience. The heartbeat of this man is to chase the sinner, restore the broken, and heal the hurting.

Twitter: @TimothyCWMcCain
Instagram: @Timothy_McCain, @OpeningEyesMinistries
Facebook: Opening Eyes Ministries
Website: www.OpeningEyesMinistries.com

CPSIA information can be obtained
at www.ICGtesting.com
Printed in the USA
LVHW04s0924200818
587502LV00019B/579/P